Richard Whately

ABOUT THE AUTHOR

Craig Parton is a partner in the firm of Price, Postel & Parma in Santa Barbara, California. He is a graduate of the California Polytechnic University (BA *Magna Cum Laude*), Simon Greenleaf School of Law (MA), and Hastings College of the Law, University of California (JD). His master's thesis was on Richard Whately.

He is a faculty member of the International Seminar in Jurisprudence and Human Rights, and Associate Director of the International Academy of Apologetics, Evangelism and Human Rights, held in Strasbourg, France.

Richard Whately

A Man for All Seasons

CANADIAN INSTITUTE FOR LAW, THEOLOGY & PUBLIC POLICY

Thy Word is a Light To My Path

First Canadian Edition, April 1997

© 1997 Canadian Institute for Law, Theology & Public Policy Inc.

Parton, Craig A. 1955 -
Whately, Richard 1787-1863

    Richard Whately: A Man for All Seasons.

    Bibliography: p.

    ISBN 1-896363-07-5

1. Whately, Richard 1787-1863
2. Biography - 19 Cent.
3. Buonaparte, Napoleon 1769-1821
4. Christianity—Evidences
5. Apologetics
6. Bible—Inspiration
7. Rhetoric

I. Title.

Publisher.
Canadian Institute for Law, Theology, and Public Policy, Inc.
7203 - 90 Avenue
Edmonton, Alberta, Canada
T6B 0P5

Printed and bound in Canada by Doppler and Sons

DEDICATION

To Dr. John Warwick Montgomery, M.
Phil., Ph.D., Th.D., avocat, théologien,
défendeur de la Foi: you have faithfully in-
structed a generation of fortunate students to
"always contend earnestly for the Faith once
delivered to the saints." Dieu Vous Garde . . .

PUBLISHER'S NOTE

Historic Doubts Relative to Napoleon Buonaparte

The text is a photolithograph of the 6th edition published by B. Fellowes, London in 1837.

The "Preface" and "Postcripts" to the Third, Seventh, Ninth and Eleventh editions are reprinted from the 4th American edition, which was based on the 11th London edition.

TABLE OF CONTENTS

Richard Whately

A Man For All Seasons

He was called, at various times, a liberal,[1] a heretic,[2] and a lover of Rome.[3] Yet the overwhelming consensus of both his colleagues and students was that "no man ever loved truth more, or more boldly followed it as he found it."[4] Richard Whately (1787-1863) was preëminently a "man for all seasons" whose rhetorical skills and controversial wit should have earned him a place of great honor in the history of apologetics. Unfortunately, though, the case is quite the opposite. Few Christians today know of the scope of Whately's contribution to the faith or of his remarkable relevance for our day.

Whately's writings spanned all the issues facing the Church in the early and middle stages of the 19th century. Whatever the issue, whether it was civil rights, church reform, biblical criticism, or Anglican theology, Whately dealt with it, invariably in a most lucid and forceful manner. Many of the greatest minds of that century knew the power of this man's influence. John Henry Newman, one of the great apologists of the 19th century, said that Whately "taught me to think and open my mind."[5] Thomas

Arnold, the famous Headmaster of Rugby and an accomplished apologist in his own right, said that if the safety and welfare of the Protestant Church depended in any degree on human instruments, "none could be found, I verily believe, in the whole empire, so likely to maintain it"[6] as Richard Whately. The rediscovery of this man of eminence is much needed.

A GATHERING STORM

The England of Richard Whately was a country at the apex of turbulence, both politically and theologically. The philosophical speculations of David Hume (1711 - 1776) and Immanuel Kant (1724 - 1804) worked to undercut confidence in Scripture as a trustworthy guide,[7] while other scholars directed a specific attack on the Bible itself. David Strauss, in his work *Leben Jesu*, directly removed the New Testament from the realm of historical inquiry and treated it as myth[8], while the work of F.C. Baur and Friedrich Schleiermacher further decimated Christian claims to a reliable and objective historical revelation in the Scripture.[9]

Coupled with this radical philosophical skepticism was a rising tide of optimism and a revived romanticism.[10] English literary endeavor reached a pinnacle during the early part of the century when such immortals as Byron, Shelley and Keats forged a reaction to the cold, rational deism of the 18th century.[11] Unfortunately, this "reaction of the heart" took a most disastrous romp through the Anglican Church.

The influence of German higher critical methods came to England initially through the efforts of men like S.T. Coleridge and Thomas Carlyle,[12] who had wisely cast it in romantic literary terms.[13]

Social factors forced the Church of England to look long and hard at its inability to minister effectively to the lower classes. A rising industrialization was bringing the multitudes into the urban areas, but the Christian church remained unable to meet the challenge. For those living in the squalor portrayed so graphically by Charles Dickens, "the church had no message."[14] Few, except the Wesleyan Methodists and Independents (Baptists, Congregationalists and Pietists), realized the tragic error that was being made in alienating the lower classes from religious life.

To a large extent, 19th century England was a land of theological confusion where the Church of England had, to a great degree, retreated from the attacks of unbelief. M.A. Crowther has shown how little 19th century Anglicanism was willing to deal with objections to the Gospel by pointing out that ordination examinations in the 1800's never asked any questions dealing with objections to the faith made by informed unbelievers.[15]

The age of Richard Whately was marked by material ease and comfort for the aristocracy and a growing intellectual skepticism. As Desmond Bowen puts it, "in almost every field of intellectual inquiry traditional viewpoints were being discarded, and among thinking men there was a general increase of uncertainty."[16] What the day called for was an apologist able to combine academic and theological acumen with evangelical fervor and social awareness. Fortunately, there was just such an individual willing and able to respond to such a call.

A SCHOLAR FOR ALL SEASONS

Born on February 1, 1787, Richard Whately was the youngest son of Dr. and Mrs. Joseph Whately. The elder Whately was both vicar of Widford and a lecturer at Gresham College.[17] Young Richard was found to possess an astonishing mathematical ability from the earliest age. By 1805 he had entered Oriel College at Oxford where he pursued his tutelage under the great Dr. Copleston. It was at Oriel that Whately would learn to harness his intellectual vigor and channel it into worthy pursuits. Soon his abilities warranted not only the earning of two degrees, but also his elevation to the post of fellow and tutor at Oriel.

Oriel College was at its intellectual height during Whately's tenure. Men like John Henry Newman, Thomas Arnold, Joseph Blanco-White, Copleston, Hinds and Whately would be given the nickname "Noetics" for their superior mental penetration and independence.[18] While at Oriel, Whately would write his famous work entitled *Logic*, which "gave a great impetus to the study of logic throughout Great Britain."[19] This work gives many early glimpses into his emphasis on reason and facts, which would play such a pivotal role in his system of apologetics.

No one was more feared as a tutor at Oriel than Whately. He combined a brilliant grasp of Greek, Latin and Hebrew with a penetrating Socratic teaching method. Always ready for a healthy exchange of ideas, Whately had little tolerance for subjective arguments and those arguments which were poorly thought through. Thomas Mozley recounts how one time the Oriel tutor "had asked some neighbors to dinner at his country parsonage, and after dinner their conversation became so disagreeable that he threw the window open, jumped out, and disappeared till late in the evening."[20]

An emphasis on a Christianity for the tough-minded often led Whately to great unpopularity as a scholar. He chastised both the Evangelical and High Church wings of the Anglican Church, charging the former with mysticism and the latter with both mysticism and irrelevance. For Whately, the majority of Christian preachers "aim at nothing, and they hit it."[21]

AN ARCHBISHOP FOR ALL SEASONS

To the surprise of all and chagrin of many, Whately was appointed Archbishop of Dublin in 1831. The master of Oriel would soon, in characteristic fashion, let his views on Catholicism and civil rights be amply known, which would create tremendous furor throughout England. Though many had felt the colorful Anglican was sent to Ireland "to destroy the Church and the faith altogether,"[22] it was certainly a case of the appointment of the right man for the right job.

One of Whately's first steps upon his appointment was his advocacy of the Catholic Emancipation Bill. This legislation would remove all civil liabilities that the Church of England had put upon the Irish Catholics. No longer would Catholics be barred from voting or holding parliamentary office. Whately would write that "to exclude any class of men from public offices, in consequence of their religion, was to make Christ's kingdom of this world, which He and His disciples had distinctly and expressly disclaimed."[23] Throughout the Archbishop's writings one sees continued reference to the necessity of protecting the civil rights of religious dissenters and maintaining a strict "two kingdoms" mentality. It was absolutely essential, said Whately, that those who are outside the faith never see a blurring of law and gospel by the state.[24]

The Archbishop incurred the severe displeasure of the English church for his stance on civil rights. When he extended his argument for civil rights to the Jewish minority, further erosion of his already waning popularity ensued. Yet Whately simply would not abandon an issue where principle was involved. He was thoroughly convinced that civil rights were not the sole privilege of the believing community.[25]

As if to add insult to injury, Whately vigorously defended the idea of a system of national education in Ireland. His idea was to educate the Catholic majority in "neither an Anglican or [sic] Catholic manner."[26] The text used for the classes would be the

Archbishop's own work entitled *Introductory Lessons on Morals and Christian Evidences*, a brilliant
work which defends what C.S. Lewis has called
"mere Christianity." While the Catholic and Jewish
Emancipation Bills would ultimately succeed, the
national education plan ran into overwhelming political opposition and was eventually allowed to die a
quiet death. Whately had a ruthless disdain for party
politics, resolving always to let Scripture rule inde-
pendently on each issue. In his own inimitable
words, "I began my career by declaring open war on
both parties."[27]

Even though Whately made tireless efforts on behalf of Catholics in the areas of civil rights and education, he was still, first and foremost, an Anglican
who stood in direct opposition to the theology of
Rome. His classic work, *The Errors of Romanism
Traced To Their Origin In Human Nature*, is a
theological masterpiece. Various shots are taken at
the priesthood, adoration of images, abuse of the con-
fessional, and, above all, the infallibility of the
Catholic Church. He put the differences between his
Anglicanism and the Roman Church in this way:

> *They* offer sacrifices for the people; *we* refer them
> to a sacrifice made by another; *they* profess to be
> the mediators through whom the Deity is to be
> addressed; *we* teach them to look to a heavenly
> Mediator, and in his name boldly to approach
> God's mercy-seat themselves; *they* study to con-
> ceal the mysteries of religion; *we* labour to make
> them known; *they* have, for the most part, hidden

sacred books, which none but a few chosen may
look into; *we* teach and exhort men to study the
word of God themselves.[28]

Whately's cogent defense of Reformation theology
was particularly necessary during his tenure as
Archbishop. From 1830-1845, the rise of the Oxford
Movement, or Tractarians as they were called, cre-
ated a virtual crisis in the Church of England. The
Tractarians, under John Henry Newman, Hurrell
Froude, John Keble, E.B. Pusey, and others desired
to see a theology that cut back, not to the Reformation, but to the early church fathers. The Oxford
Movement boasted that "Luther is dead, but Hilde-
brand and Loyola are alive."[29] Eventually the Tractarians would move completely into the arms of
Rome, and would take many Anglicans with them.
Unfortunately, Whately's controversial social stands
served to undercut the impact of his lucid and powerful critique of Catholicism and the Tractarians.

But the tutor of Oriel did not limit his pen to incisive polemics against Anglo-Catholicism and High
Church Anglican mysticism. He felt that the rising
tide of Evangelicalism within the Church of England
had left behind the crucial anchor of systematic theology.[30] With its lack of emphasis on the intellect
and theology, this growing movement called forth a
spirited response from Whately. The Christian religion, said the Archbishop, rests on the facts of history.
He reiterated the fact that the faith rested on evidence, which must be weighed by the use of human
reason.[31] Those who reject the historic confessions of

the faith and the theology of the Reformers, relying instead on being "moved by the Holy Spirit may fairly be asked to prove this by the display of some sensible miracle."[32] Evangelical piety led to that deplorable state where its possessors "imagine that they have attained a very high degree of Christian perfection."[33] Samuel Butler would portray the negative side of Victorian piety with devastating literary force in *The Way Of All Flesh*, while Whately took his theological scalpel to Evangelicalism's degradation of the historical objectivity of the Christian faith.

Though he remained an Anglican to his death, church historians have found it virtually impossible to categorize Whately's theology. His respect for the creeds of the Christian church and his position as Archbishop certainly lend support for his inclusion as a member of the traditional High Church wing. Yet Whately deplored the church's lack of reform and publicly challenged the religious practices of the High Churchmen. His writings against Evangelical Pietists and their accompanying Calvinist theology, along with a total adherence to an inerrant Word of God and scriptural (i.e., Christocentric) theology argue for placing him directly in the stream of the Lutheran Reformation. All that Thomas Arnold could say about Whately was that "there does not live a truer Christian."[34]

AN APOLOGIST FOR ALL SEASONS

It would be a tragedy to see Whately only as an outstanding theologian and scholar, since his direct contribution to apologetics is immense. As an apologist, he was an "evidentialist" of the purest sort. In his classic work on the use of evidence in defending Christian truth, he writes:

> The Christian religion was brought in, in opposition to all these [false religions], by means of the reasons given - the evidence, which convinced the early Christians that the religion did truly come from God. It must therefore be the duty of Christians to learn what the evidence is.[35]

One should not be content with simply having a reason to believe but must also be able to articulate that reason within the unbelieving community. Faith not resting on evidence, says Whately, is pure and simple "credulity."[36]

The Archbishop addressed several areas of particular apologetical interest. In his work entitled *Essays On Some Of The Difficulties In The Writings Of St.Paul,* Whately gives clear and concise guidelines for dealing with alleged contradictions in the Bible. First, one must know the "general drift and design"[37] of the passage in question. Second, there should be a solid knowledge of the original meaning of the words in the passage.[38] Third, an understanding of figurative, analogical and literary forms will help elucidate any remaining difficulties.[39]

Undoubtedly, Whately's greatest apologetical effort is contained in a small book entitled *Historic Doubts Relative To Napoleon Buonaparte.* John

Warwick Montgomery has aptly labeled it a *tour de force* in apologetical literature[40]

David Hume's arguments against the miraculous had a seemingly devastating effect on the Christian church of the day. According to the Scottish philosopher, a miracle is a violation of the laws of nature and such laws have been established by unalterable experience. Since a wise man proportions his belief to the evidence, the proof against the miraculous is as "entire as any argument from experience can possibly be imagined."[41] For Hume, every alleged miracle is refuted by "an infinite number of witnesses."[42]

In *Historic Doubts Relative To Napoleon Buonaparte*, Whately applies Hume's "laws" to the life of Napoleon Buonaparte. The Archbishop's tongue-in-cheek conclusion is that there is no credible evidence that Napoleon ever existed. This conclusion is reached even though Napoleon was actually alive at the time of the book's publication!

Whately claims that no one was assigned such dissimilar characteristics as Napoleon. The French genius is always painted as either a great liberator or a butcherous villain, depending on the person writing the account. He is said to have won astounding victories and survived overwhelming odds. Does this not, asks Whately, violate our common experience?[43] All the "sources" of information on the life of Napoleon have a vested interest in making him look either foolish or brilliant, but no one has asked the more fundamental question as to whether Buonaparte even exists!

Even eyewitnesses carry no evidential weight, says Whately, since one already knows that no man could possibly accomplish the feats attributed to Napoleon. The whole story is not "conformable to experience."[44] As if to put a last lance through the bleeding Hume, he concludes:

> If then philosophers, who reject every wonderful story that is maintained by priests, are yet found ready to believe *everything else*, however improbable, they will surely lay themselves open to the accusation brought against them of being unduly prejudiced against whatever relates to religion.[45]

Historic Doubts Relative To Napoleon Buonaparte makes the important point that unbelievers cannot simply dismiss historic Christian claims on philosophical grounds and then refuse to deal with the eyewitness evidence contained in the documents. All of the objections raised against the reliability of the Biblical material can be turned around and used in a most alarming way on all scholarship. The result is that all knowledge of history will collapse in a Humeian pile, a result which Whately doubts that many are willing to accept.

After successfully annihilating Hume's argument against the miraculous, the Archbishop of Dublin turned his apologetical pen to the rising tide of criticism aimed at the Scripture. German scholarship in mid-Victorian England had, as Kenneth Scott Latourette pointed out, reduced the Gospel to mere ideas.[46] The critics became obsessed with "what actually happened" in the New Testament. Unfortunately, the inevitable conclusion was that in getting at "what actually happened" the investigators forced the Biblical material into their own procrustean bed of higher critical presuppositions.

It is little wonder that Whately again saw a prime opportunity to use the methods of Christianity's critics against them in an even more hilarious manner. *Historic Certainties Respecting The Early History of America* claims to be written by a Reverend Aristarchus Newlight. The Rev. Newlight (alias Whately) claims also to be a "Doctor of Philosophy at the University of Giessen, a corresponding member of the theophilanthropic and pantisocratical societies of Leipsic, and the late professor of all religions."[47]

This riotous volume is dedicated to "the learned and enlightened public of Europe and America, specially to those eminent critics, at home and abroad, whose labours upon Jewish History I have humbly made my model."[48] Newlight claims to have recovered the *Chronicles Of The Land Of Ecnarf*, which tell a simple narrative of a foreign land. The good Reverend then proceeds to give his "interpretation" of the story in order to "enlighten" the reader. Such enlightenment consists of showing how the *Chronicles* give the long lost connection between Palestine and America. This "clear connection" is found by showing that the original name of our continent was "Noah". Of course, any piece of the original document that does not agree with Newlight's presuppositional bias is immediately labeled a "tangled web."[49]

Though not as well known as his work on Napoleon, *Historic Certainties Respecting The Early History Of America* scores a direct hit on the higher critical methods of men like Baur and Strauss. By showing how some attempt to force "history" out of mythology, Whately makes the point that others do just the opposite when they refuse to allow an historical document to speak for itself.

A CHRISTIAN FOR ALL SEASONS

As Thomas Arnold said, Richard Whately is one of the truly great examples of one whose "intellectual part of his nature keeps pace with the spiritual."[50] The overwhelming need of the day was for someone willing and able to deal intelligently with the objections of non-Christians to the claims of historic Christianity, while also embracing a vibrant personal faith. The Victorian age, in the words of L.E. Elliott-Binns, was supremely an "age of doubt and conflict."[51] A gathering storm of philosophical and theological attacks from within and without the faith was rarely met with a timely apologetic. Both High Church Anglicanism and Evangelicalism presented different versions of escapism for the 19th century English Christian. Few were available to "stand in the gap" with the likes of Hume, Strauss, Baur and others.

In addition to possessing a healthy hunger for dialogue with unbelief, the master of Oriel was that rare combination of a scholar and a communicator. Like Martin Luther, Whately was a determined and disciplined thinker and writer who never lost his love for the common man. One is constantly amazed at the clarity, simplicity and tremendous force of Whately's writings. It is indeed unfortunate that this 19th century C.S. Lewis was greatly ignored in his own day and is virtually forgotten in ours.

The love of truth and, above all, the centrality of the Gospel, relentlessly drove the Archbishop of Dublin to embrace and aggressively advocate unpopular themes. Unlike our modern day "super preachers," Whately cared little for popularity and less for gathering "Whatelyites."[52] His constant message was that in the Scriptures alone one may find saving truth, and once it is found one must champion it at all costs.

This Anglican apologist had no tolerance for those Christians who espoused a dichotomy between heart and mind, usually to the detriment of the mind. He saw clearly that apologetical approaches which solely stressed "what Jesus has done for me" sadly lack the force and sanction of the evidential flavor of the New Testament, nor do they command serious consideration from unbelievers faced with a variety of religious options.

Though a man of immense intellectual abilities, Whately remained throughout his life pleasantly approachable, even if somewhat eccentric. Stories about the Archbishop abounded throughout England, no doubt spurred by his "utter disregard for customs and regulations."[53] From his casual tutorial style to his dogs which climbed trees, Whately was always delightfully unpredictable!

Richard Whately was "a man for all seasons." Like Thomas More, he located himself at those points of principle and truth from which no man of Scripture should be moved. He is eternally relevant because his life was fused with the heart of God's Word, namely the person and work of our Lord Jesus Christ. The defense of the Scripture and of the saving Gospel it contains guarantees that one will have truly built upon a most sure foundation. Richard Whately was a most pure and appealing example of this truth.

---

[1]L.E. Elliott-Binns, *Religion In The Victorian Era* (Greenwich, Conn.: Seabury Press, 1953), p. 47.

[2]Otto Pfleiderer, *The Development of Theology In Germany Since Kant And Its Progress In Great Britain Since 1825,* trans. J. Frederick Smith (London: Swan Sonnenschein and Co., 1890), p. 369.

[3]E.J. Whately, *The Life and Correspondence of Archbishop Whately,* Vol. I (London: Longmans, Green and Co., 1866), pp. 102-105. Oddly enough, Evangelicals and Catholics are now in a mad rush to form ecumenical unions. See C. Colson & R.J. Neuhaus, eds., *Evangelicals & Catholics Together: Toward a Christian Mission* (Dallas: Word, 1995).

[4]John Tulloch, *Movements Of Religious Thought In Great Britain During The Nineteenth Century* (New York: Charles Scribner's Sons, 1885), p. 52.

[5]John Henry Cardinal Newman, *Apologia Pro Vita Sua,* ed. Charles Harold (London: Longmans, Green and Co., 1947), p. 10. Few need to write apologies for their lives but then, again, few are those who convert from Anglicanism to Roman Ca-

tholicism. Newman is a favorite among Catholics for his de-
fection, and this literary classic is a must for those interested in
Whately's most renowned pupil.

[6]A.P. Stanley, *The Life And Correspondence of Thomas
Arnold*, 9th ed. (Boston: James R. Osgood & Co., 1871), p.
275. Arnold's son, Matthew (1822-1888), was a literary giant
in his own right, even though he accepted most of his father's
destructive views concerning the authority of Holy Writ.

[7]Roland Stromberg, *European Intellectual History Since
1784*, 3rd ed.(Englewood Cliffs, New Jersey: Prentice-Hall,
1981), p. 30. Because knowledge only constructs reality for
Kant and does not correspond to reality, one cannot know the
way things are in themselves. Rational processes must yield to
a subjective reality. Kant ultimately jettisoned any hope of
proving the existence of God in any rational sense. *Ibid.*, p. 31.

[8]M.A. Crowther, *Church Embattled: Religious Controversy
In Mid-Victorian England* (Hamden, Conn.: Archon Books,
1970), p. 44. Strauss taught that the Hegelian dialectic is
found in Scripture and that Scripture was reliable to the degree
that it taught Hegelianism. See Charles Hodge, *Systematic
Theology*, Vol. 1, (Grand Rapids: Eerdmans, 1979), p. 6.

[9]Pfleiderer, pp. 44, 200. Schleiermacher eventually moved
into a position of total subjectivism and emotional mysticism
with regard to theological questions, concluding that religion is
only a "feeling of cosmic dependence." See also Norman
Geisler, *Miracles And Modern Thought* (Richardson, TX:
Probe, 1982), pp. 137-138.

[10]John Warwick Montgomery, *The Suicide of Christian
Theology* (Minneapolis: Bethany House Publishers, 1981), p.
28. The 19th century critics of the Bible endeavored "to re-do
the biblical revelation in the image of the 19th century Zeit-
geist, and where it did not fit, they made it fit . . . ."

[11]William Vaughn Moody, *A History Of English Literature* (New York: Charles Scribner's Sons, 1902), p. 298.

[12]*Ibid.*, pp. 296-299. Coleridge developed his own species of Biblical criticism by asserting that whatever in the Bible touches the individual is "of the Lord" and the rest is mystery. Tulloch, p. 26.

[13] Pfleiderer, pp. 307-316. Carlyle said that he learned to disregard his "barren logical intellect," being careful to point out that he was "endlessly indebted to Goethe." Tulloch, p. 194.

[14]S.C. Carpenter, *Church & People, 1789-1889: A History Of The Church Of England From William Wilberforce to "Lux Mundi"*(London: Macmillan & Co., 1933), p. 27.

[15]Crowther, p. 229. Query: whether ordination examinations today require any appreciable level of competency to be displayed in the field of apologetics.

[16]Desmond Bowen, *The Idea Of the Victorian Church* (Montreal: McGill University Press, 1968), p. 142.

[17]E.J. Whately, pp. 1-4.

[18]For the classic study on Oriel's preeminent position within Oxford during Whately's tenure, see Thomas Mozley, *Reminiscences Chiefly of Oriel College And The Oxford Movement*, Vol. I (Boston: Houghton Mifflin & Co., 1882), p. 20.

[19] As to the revival of interest in logic under Whately's Donship at Oxford, see William John Fitzpatrick, *Memoirs of Richard Whately*, Vol. I (London: Richard Bentley Publishers, 1864), p. 46. Fitzpatrick provides valuable insight into the

connection between Whately and the thought of Francis Bacon at pp. 325-326.

[20] Mozley, p. 268.

[21]*Ibid.*, p. 272. For a devastating critique of the impact of early nineteenth century Anglicanism's connection to the privileged classes of England, see S.L. Ollard, *What England Owes To The Oxford Movement* (London: A.R. Mowbray & Co., 1923), p. 38ff.

[22]Mozley, p. 269.

[23]E.J. Whately, p. 74. For a revealing look at the personal financial sacrifices Archbishop Whately made on behalf of destitute Irish Catholics after the potato famine of 1846, see R.A. Soloway, *Prelates And People: Ecclesiastical Social Thought In England 1783-1852* (London: Routledge and Kegan Paul, 1969), p. 163.

[24]Richard Whately, *Miscellaneous Remains From The Commonplace Book Of Richard Whately, D.D.*, ed. E.J. Whately (London: Longmans, Green and Co., 1864), p.194. C.S. Lewis makes the same point when discussing the dangers of national repentance in his work *God In The Dock* (Grand Rapids: Eerdmans, 1970), p. 189ff.

[25]Richard Whately, *Charges & Other Tracts* (London: B. Fellowes, 1836), pp.475-477. This work covers a variety of topics with most emphasis being given to the need to protect the civil rights of the Jewish minority in England—see esp., pp. 427-477. For a thoughtful discussion of the importance of grounding human rights activity on a defensible and revelational basis, see John Warwick Montgomery, *Human Rights And Human Dignity* (Edmonton: Canadian Institute for Law, Theology and Public Policy, 1995).

[26]E.J. Whately, p. 137.

[27]*Ibid.*, p. 69.

[28]Richard Whately, *The Errors Of Romanism Traced To Their Origin In Human Nature* (London: B. Fellowes, 1830), p. 109. For an excellent discussion of the English Reformation, the Anglican Church as the *via media* and its theological synthesis of Luther, Calvin and Zwingli, see Philip Schaff, *The Creeds of Christendom,* Vol. I, (Grand Rapids: Baker Books, 1983), esp. pp. 607-611 for a summation of the contribution of Richard Hooker to Anglican theology.

[29]Bowen, p. 49. Hurrel Froude summed up the prevailing sentiment of the Oxford Movement with respect to the Protestant Reformation: "Really, I hate the Reformation and the Reformers more and more." See Horton Davies, *Worship And Theology In England from Watts and Wesley to Maurice, 1690-1850,* Vol. III (Princeton: Princeton University Press, 1961), p. 255.

[30]Henry Offley Wakeman, *An Introduction To The History Of The Church of England*, 7th ed. (London: Rivingtons, 1904), p. 450. Unfortunately, Anglicanism has not been known for its systematic theologians and cannot boast of giving birth to giants like Mueller and Pieper (Lutheran) or Berkhof and Hodge (Reformed).

[31]Richard Whately, *Introductory Lessons On Morals And Christian Evidences* (Cambridge: John Bartlett, 1856), p. 193. For superb modern presentations of this evidential approach to apologetics, see John Warwick Montgomery, *Faith Founded On Fact: Essays In Evidential Apologetics* (Nashville: Thomas Nelson Publishers, 1978) and Wilbur Smith, *Therefore Stand: A Plea For A Vigorous Apologetic In the Present Crisis of Evangelical Christianity* (Boston: W.A. Wilde Co., 1950).

[32]*Ibid.*, pp. 103-104. Luther puts it nicely: "This is why we should and must constantly insist on the fact that God does not intend to deal with us otherwise than through His external Word and Sacraments. Everything that is exalted as Spirit without this Word and Sacraments is of the Devil." Ewald Plass, *What Luther Says*, Vol. II (St. Louis: Concordia Publishing House, 1959), p. 915.

[33]Richard Whately, *Essays On Some Of The Difficulties In The Writings of St.Paul* (London: B. Fellowes, 1828), p. 295.

[34]Stanley, p. 275. For a fascinating study of the impact of the Lutheran Reformation on Anglican theology, liturgy and worship, see the remarkable story of Robert Barnes found in Neelak S. Tjernagel's *Lutheran Martyr* (Milwaukee: Northwestern Publishing House, 1982). Tjernagel's well-documented conclusion is that while a Reformed interpretation of the Sacrament of the Altar was to find its way into the Thirty-Nine Articles, the fact of the matter is that the "doctrinal and liturgical foundations of the Anglican Church remained Lutheran even though succeeding generations might give them a Calvinistic color and interpretation." *Id.* At p. 168. Tjernagel's work carefully documents the influence of the English Lutheran Robert Barnes on the doctrinal formulations of the Anglican Church and concludes that the substance of the Lutheran Augsburg Confession became the basis of formal Anglican theology. *Id.* At pp. 167-8.

[35]R. Whately, *Introductory Lessons,* p. 193. Christianity's emphasis on evidence and fact explains its historic attraction for the legally trained mind. William Blackstone, Matthew Hale, Simon Greenleaf, Thomas Erskine, Sir Norman Anderson, Lord Hailsham, and John Warwick Montgomery are but a few examples of legal scholars who have found the evidence for Christian faith compelling. See, for example, Simon Greenleaf, *The Testimony Of The Evangelists*, contained as an Appendix in John Warwick Montgomery's *Law Above The Law*

(Minneapolis: Bethany House Publishers, 1975): and Lord Hailsham, *The Door Wherein I Went* (London: Collins, 1975). Lord Hailsham is a former Lord High Chancellor of England. See also Ross Clifford, *Leading Lawyers' Case for the Resurrection* (Edmonton: Canadian Institute for Law, Theology and Public Policy, 1996).

[36]R.Whately, *Introductory Lessons,* p. 196. "Islam," says Whately, "was propagated, not by evidence, but by the sword."

[37]R. Whately, *Essays*, pp. 202-203.

[38]*Ibid.,* p. 204.

[39]*Ibid.,* p. 219. For a *magnum opus* on alleged contradictions in the Bible, see Gleason Archer, *Encyclopedia Of Bible Difficulties* (Grand Rapids: Zondervan, 1982).

[40] John Warwick Montgomery, *The Suicide of Christian Theology* (Minneapolis: Bethany Fellowship, 1970), p. 43.

[41]David Hume, *An Inquiry Concerning Human Understanding,* ed. C.W. Hendel (New York: Bobbs-Merrill, 1955), sec. 10. pt. 1 p. 122. For an incisive dissection of Hume's argument against the miraculous as being completely circular, see C.S. Lewis, *Miracles: A Preliminary Study* (New York: Macmillan Publishing Company, 1977).

[42]Edwin A Burtt, *The English Philosophers From Bacon to Mill* (New York: Random House, 1939), p. 661.

[43]Richard Whately, *Historic Doubts Relative To Napoleon Buonaparte* (New York: Robert Carter & Bros., 1880), p. 16.

[44]*Ibid.,* p. 43.

[45]*Ibid.,* p. 58.

[46]Kenneth Scott Latourette, *A History Of Christianity*, Vol. II (New York: Harper & Row, 1975), p. 1128.

[47]Richard Whately, *Historic Certainties Respecting The Early History Of America* (New York: Robert Carter & Bros., 1880), preface.

[48]*Ibid.*, preface.

[49]*Ibid.*, p. 129. For a hilarious and more modern literary exposé as to how presuppositional bias can destroy hermeneutical integrity, see Frederick Crews, *The Pooh Perplex* (New York: E.P. Dutton & Co., 1963). For example, Crews, writing under an ecclesiastical pseudonym, pens one chapter entitled "The Sacramental Meaning of Winnie-The-Pooh."

[50]Stanley, p. 275.

[51]L.E. Elliott-Binns, *The Development Of English Theology In The Later Nineteenth Century* (London: Longmans, Green and Co., 1952), p. 7.

[52]E.J. Whately, Vol. II, p. 47. "No. I'll have no Whately-ites! I think I could before now, if I had been so disposed, have raised myself into the leader of a party—that is, induced a certain number of asses to change their panniers. But I have no such ambition."

[53]E.J. Whately, Vol. I, p. 38. This is a comprehensive biography of Whately done by his daughter. It contains a wealth of information on the personal, political and theological opinions of the Archbishop as well as a plethora of personal correspondence.

Annotated Bibliography of Select Writings of Richard Whately

Note: The edition cited is the most widely available, not necessarily the earliest.

Apostolic Succession Reconsidered. London: Longmans, Green and Co., 1912.

Whately's typically independent view on the apostolic succession of the episcopacy is outlined here (see pp. 135ff especially).

Charges And Other Tracts. London: B.Fellowes, 1836.

Covers a variety of topics, with most emphasis being given to the civil rights of the Jewish minority in England (see especially pp. 427-477).

Controversy Between Tract XC And The Oxford Tutors, The. London: Howe and Parsons, 1841.

A devastating reply to Newman's famous "Tract XC." Effectively dealt with the argument that the 39 Articles could be harmonized with Catholic theology.

Easy Lessons On Reasoning. 3rd ed. Boston: James Munroe and Co., 1852.
> Contains a chapter on the role of induction in the reasoning process (see pp. 163ff).

Elements of Logic, The. 9th ed. London: Longmans, Green and Co., 1865.
> A standard textbook on the subject, this volume presents Whately's distinction between statements of logic and statements of history (see especially pp. 9-35 and 160-187).

Errors Of Romanism Traced To Their Origin In Human Nature, The. London: B. Fellowes, 1830.
> Whately's exposé of Catholicism, written with a wary eye towards the rising Tractarian Movement.

Essays On Some Of The Difficulties In The Writings of Saint Paul. London: B. Fellowes, 1828.
> A lucid work that deals with such issues as election, double predestination, perserverance of the saints, and alleged contradictions in Scripture.

Historic Certainties Respecting The Early History Of America. New York: Robert Carter and Brothers, 1880.

Historic Doubts Relative to Napoleon Buonaparte. New York: Robert Carter and Brothers, 1880.
> Known as Whately's apologetical *tour de force*.

Introductory Lessons On Morals And Christian Evidences. Cambridge: John Bartlett, 1856.
A powerful case is argued for the historicity of Christian claims.

Kingdom of Christ Delineated, The. New York: Robert Carter and Brothers, 1854.
Whately's best work on the issue of the civil rights of unbelievers.

Miscellaneous Remains From The Commonplace Book of Richard Whately, D. D., ed. E.J. Whately. London: Longmans and Green, 1864.
Includes comments by Whately on subjects ranging from Islam, where he points out the circularity of Islamic apologetical approaches (p. 96), to marriage, where one is told that "if you are crossed in love, whether by being jilted or otherwise, resolve not to marry or engage yourself for a year and a day" (p. 105). Typical of the chapters is the one entitled, "Of Frogs And Toads," where one learns the hidden secret of the ages, that "frogs delight excessively in being scratched with the end of a stick" (p. 115).

Rhetoric. London: B.Fellowes, 1828.
A series of lessons on the art of composition and persuasion. A companion volume to *The Elements Of Logic*.

Search After Infallibility, The. Dublin: Hodges and Smith, 1847.

Points out the theological suicide which occurs when ecclesiastical infallibility replaces Scriptural authority.

Sermons On Various Subjects Delivered In Several Churches In The City Of Dublin And In Other Parts Of The Diocese. London: B. Fellowes, 1835.
For a comprehensive view of the role of an historical resurrection in Whately's theology, see pp. 157-166.

Thoughts And Apophthegms From The Writings Of Archbishop Whately. Philadelphia: Lindsay and Blakiston, 1856.

Editor, *View Of The Evidences Of Christianity, A,* by William Paley. New York: James Miller, 1856.
Whately did both the introduction and the notes to this apologetical classic. His understanding of the use of General Revelation (Romans 1) in the apologetical task is elucidated in the introduction.

View Of The Scripture Revelations Respecting Good And Evil Angels, A. Philadelphia: Lindsay and Blakiston, 1856.
Contains a fascinating chapter on demon-possession, along with Whately's detailed study of the work of Satan as revealed in the Scriptures.

HISTORIC

DOUBTS

NAPOLEON BUONAPARTE.

———◆———

" Is not the same reason available in theology and in politics? ....
Will you follow truth but to a certain point?"

Burke's Vindication of Natural Society.

SIXTH EDITION.

LONDON:

B. FELLOWES, LUDGATE STREET.

1837.

LONDON:

R. CLAY, PRINTER, BREAD-STREET-HILL.

PREFACE.

Several of the readers of this little work have derived much amusement from the mistakes of others respecting its nature and object. It has been by some represented as a serious attempt to inculcate universal scepticism; while others have considered it as a jeu d'esprit, &c. The Author does not, however, design to entertain his readers with accounts of the mistakes which have arisen respecting it; because many of them, he is convinced, would be received with incredulity; and he could not, without an indelicate exposure of individuals, verify his anecdotes.

But some sensible readers have complained of the difficulty of determining *what* they are to believe. Of the existence of Buonaparte, indeed, they remained fully convinced; nor, if it were left doubtful, would any important results ensue; but if they can give no *satisfactory reason* for their conviction, how can they know, it is asked, that they may not be mistaken as to other points of greater consequence, on which they are no less fully convinced, but on which all men are *not* agreed? The Author has accordingly been solicited to endeavor to frame some canons which may furnish a standard for determining what evidence is to be received.

This he conceives to be impracticable, except to that extent to which it is accomplished by a sound system of Logic; including under that title, a portion—that which relates to the "Laws of Evidence"—of what is sometimes treated of under the head of "Rhetoric." But the full and complete accomplish-

ment of such an object would confer on man the un-
attainable attribute of infallibility.

But the difficulty complained of, he conceives to
arise, in many instances, from men's *misstating the
grounds of their own conviction.* They are convinced, indeed, and perhaps with very sufficient reason; but they imagine this reason to be a different one
from what it is. The evidence to which they have as-
sented is applied to their minds in a different manner
from that in which they believe it is—and suppose it
ought to be—applied. And when challenged to defend
and justify their own belief, they feel at a loss, because they are attempting to maintain a position
which is not in fact that in which their force lies.

For a development of the nature, the consequences, and the remedies of this mistake, the reader
is referred to "Hinds on Inspiration," pp. 30-46. If
such a development is to be found in any earlier
works, the Author of the following pages at least has
never chanced to meet with any attempt of the kind.[*]

It has been objected, again, by some persons of no
great logical accuracy of thought, that as there would
not be any *moral blame* imputable to one who should
seriously disbelieve, or doubt, the existence of Buonaparte, so neither is a rejection of the Scripture histories to be considered as implying anything morally
culpable.

The same objection, such as it is, would apply
equally to many of the Parables of the New Testa-

---

[*] See *Elements of Rhetoric*, p. i. ch. 2, § 4.

ment. It might be said, for instance, that as a woman who should decline taking the trouble of searching for her lost "piece of silver," or a merchant who should neglect making an advantageous purchase of a "goodly pearl," would be guilty of no moral wrong, it must follow that there is nothing morally wrong in neglecting to reclaim a lost sinner, or in rejecting the Gospel, &c.

But any man of common sense readily perceives that the force of these parables consists in the circumstance that men do *not* usually show this carelessness about temporal goods; and, therefore, are guilty of gross and culpable *inconsistency*, if they are comparatively careless about what is far more important.

So, also, in the present case. If any man's mind were so constituted as to reject the same evidence in *all* matters alike—if, for instance, he really doubted or disbelieved the existence of Buonaparte, and considered the Egyptian pyramids as fabulous, because, forsooth, he had no "experience" of the erection of such huge structures, and *had* experience of travellers telling huge lies—he would be regarded, perhaps, as very silly, or as insane, but not as morally culpable. But if (as is intimated in the concluding sentence of this work) a man is influenced in one case by objections which, in another case, he would deride, then he stands convicted of being unfairly biassed by his prejudices.

It is only necessary to add, that as this work first appeared in the year 1819, many things are spoken of in the present tense, to which the past would now be applicable.

A Postscript was added to the third edition, which was published soon after the accounts of Buonaparte's death reached us; and another at the time of the supposed removal of his remains. A third, in reference to more recent occurrences, was added to the ninth edition.

HISTORIC DOUBTS

RELATIVE TO

NAPOLEON BUONAPARTE.

———◆———

LONG as the public attention has been occupied by the extraordinary Personage from whose ambition we are supposed to have so narrowly escaped, the subject seems to have lost scarcely any thing of its interest. We are still occupied in recounting the exploits, discussing the character, inquiring into the present situation, and even conjecturing as to the future prospects of Napoleon Buonaparte.

Nor is this at all to be wondered at, if we consider the very extraordinary nature of those exploits, and of that character; their greatness and extensive importance, as well as the un-exampled strangeness of the events, and also, that strong additional stimulant, the mysterious

uncertainty that hangs over the character of
the man.   If it be doubtful whether any history
(exclusive of such as is avowedly fabulous) ever
attributed to its hero such a series of wonderful
achievements compressed into so small a space of
time, it is certain that to no one were ever
assigned so many dissimilar characters.

It is true indeed that party prejudices have
drawn a favourable and an unfavourable por-
trait, of almost every eminent man ; but amidst
all the diversities of colouring, something of
the same general outline is always distinguish-
able.   And even the virtues in the one description, bear some resemblance to the vices of
another ; rashness, for instance, will be called
courage, or courage, rashness ; heroic firmness,
and obstinate pride, will correspond in the two
opposite descriptions : and in some leading fea-
tures, both will agree.   Neither the friends nor
the enemies, of Philip of Macedon, or of Julius
Cæsar, ever questioned their COURAGE or their
MILITARY SKILL.

With Buonaparte however it has been otherwise.   This obscure Corsican adventurer, a
man, according to some, of extraordinary talents and courage, according to others, of
very moderate abilities, and a rank coward,
advanced rapidly in the French army, obtained

a high command, gained a series of important
victories, and, elated by success, embarked
in an expedition against Egypt; which was
planned and conducted, according to some,
with the most consummate skill, according to
others, with the utmost wildness and folly:
he was unsuccessful however; and leaving the
army of Egypt in a very distressed situation,
he returned to France, and found the nation,
or at least the army, so favourably disposed
towards him, that he was enabled, with the
utmost ease, to overthrow the existing government, and obtain for himself the supreme
power; at first under the modest appellation
of Consul, but afterwards with the more sound-
ing title of Emperor. While in possession of
this power, he overthrew the most powerful
coalitions of the other European states against
him; and though driven from the sea by the
British fleets, overran nearly the whole continent, triumphant; finishing a war, not un-
frequently, in a single campaign, he entered
the capitals of most of the hostile potentates,
deposed and created kings at his pleasure, and
appeared the virtual sovereign of the chief
part of the continent, from the frontiers of
Spain to those of Russia. Even those countries we find him invading with prodigious

armies, defeating their forces, penetrating to their capitals, and threatening their total subjugation. But at Moscow his progress is stopped : a winter of unusual severity, cooperating with the efforts of the Russians, totally destroys his enormous host; and the German sovereigns throw off the yoke, and combine to oppose him. He raises another vast army, which is also ruined at Leipsic : and again another, with which, like a second Antæus, he for some time maintains himself in France ; but is finally defeated, deposed, and banished to the island of Elba, of which the sovereignty is conferred on him. Thence he returns, in about nine months, at the head of 600 men, to attempt the deposition of King Louis, who had been peaceably recalled ; the French nation declare in his favour, and he is reinstated without a struggle. He raises another great army to oppose the allied powers, which is totally defeated at Waterloo : he is a second time deposed, surrenders to the British, and is placed in confinement at the island of St. Helena. Such is the outline of the eventful history presented to us ; in the detail of which, however, there is almost every conceivable variety of statement ; while the motives and conduct of the chief actor are involved in still greater doubt, and the subject of still more eager controversy.

In the midst of these controversies, the preliminary question, concerning the *existence* of this extraordinary personage, seems never to have occurred to any one as a matter of doubt; and to show even the smallest hesitation in admitting it, would probably be regarded as an excess of scepticism; on the ground that this point has always been taken for granted by the disputants on all sides, being indeed implied by the very nature of their disputes.

But is it in fact found that *undisputed* points are always such as have been the most carefully examined as to the evidence on which they rest? that facts or principles which are taken for granted, without controversy, as the common basis of opposite opinions, are always themselves established on sufficient grounds? On the contrary, is not any such fundamental point, from the very circumstance of its being taken for granted at once, and the attention drawn off to some other question, likely to be admitted on insufficient evidence, and the flaws in that evidence overlooked? Experience will teach us that such instances often occur: witness the well-known anecdote of the Royal Society; to whom King Charles II. proposed as a question, whence it is that a vessel of water receives no addition of weight from a live fish being put into it, though it does, if the fish be dead. Various solutions, of great ingenuity, were proposed, discussed, objected to, and defended; nor was it till they had been long bewildered in the inquiry, that it occurred to them to *try the experiment ;* by which they at once ascertained, that the phenomenon which they were striving to account for,—which was the acknowledged basis and substratum, as it were, of their debates,—had no existence but in the invention of the witty monarch.*

Another instance of the same kind is so very remarkable that I cannot forbear mentioning it. It was objected to the system of Copernicus when first brought forward, that if the

---

* " A report is spread, (says Voltaire in one of his works,) " that there is, in some country or other, a giant as big as a " mountain ; and men presently fall to hot disputing concerning " the precise length of his nose, the breadth of his thumb, and " other particulars, and anathematize each other for heterodoxy " of belief concerning them.   In the midst of all, if some bold " sceptic ventures to hint a doubt as to the existence of this " giant, all are ready to join against him and tear him to " pieces."   This looks almost like a prophetic allegory relating to the gigantic Napoleon.

earth turned on its axis as he represented,
a stone dropped from the summit of a tower
would not fall at the foot of it, but at a great
distance to the west; *in the same manner as
a stone dropped from the mast-head of a ship
in full sail, does not fall at the foot of the mast,
but towards the stern.* To this it was answered,
that a stone being a *part* of the earth obeys
the same laws, and moves with it; whereas,
it is no part of the ship; of which consequently
its motion is independent. This solution was
admitted by some, but opposed by others;
and the controversy went on with spirit; nor
was it till *one hundred years* after the death of
Copernicus, that the experiment being tried, it
was ascertained that the stone thus dropped
from the head of the mast, *does* fall at the foot
of it!*

Let it be observed that I am not now im-
pugning any one particular point; but merely
shewing generally, that what is *unquestioned*
is not necessarily unquestionable; since men
will often, at the very moment when they are
accurately sifting the evidence of some disputed
point, admit hastily, and on the most insufficient

* Οὕτως ἀταλαίπωρος τοῖς πολλοῖς ἡ ζήτησις τῆς ἀληθείας,
καὶ ἐπὶ τὰ ἕτοιμα μᾶλλον τρέπονται. Thucyd. b. i. c. 20.

grounds, what they have been accustomed to see taken for granted.

The celebrated Hume* has pointed out also the readiness with which men believe, on very slight evidence, any story that pleases their imagination by its admirable and marvellous character. Such hasty credulity, however, as he well remarks, is utterly unworthy of a philosophical mind ; which should rather suspend its judgment the more, in proportion to the strangeness of the account ; and yield to none but the most decisive and unimpeachable proofs.

Let it then be allowed us, as is surely reasonable, just to inquire, with respect to the extraordinary story I have been speaking of, on what evidence we believe it. We shall be told that it is *notorious ;* i. e. in plain English, it is very *much talked about.* But as the generality of those who talk about Buonaparte

---

*. " With what greediness are the miraculous accounts of " travellers received, their descriptions of sea and land mon- " sters, their relations of wonderful adventures, strange men, " and uncouth manners." *Hume's Essay on Miracles,* p. 179. 12mo. ; p. 185. 8vo. 1767 ; p. 117. 8vo. 1817.

N. B.   In order to give every possible facility of reference, three editions of Hume's Essays have been generally employed ; a 12mo. London, 1756, and two 8vo. editions.

do not even pretend to speak from *their own authority*, but merely to repeat what they have casually heard, we cannot reckon them as in any degree witnesses ; but must allow ninety-nine hundredths of what we are told, to be mere hear-say, which would not be at all the more worthy of credit even if it were repeated by ten times as many more. As for those who profess to have *personally known* Napoleon Buonaparte, and to have *themselves witnessed* his transactions, I write not for them : *if any such there be,* who are inwardly conscious of the truth of all they relate, I have nothing to say to them, but to beg that they will be tolerant and charitable towards their neighbours, who have not the same means of ascertaining the truth ; and who may well be excused for remaining doubtful about such extraordinary events, till most unanswerable proofs shall be adduced. " I would not have believed such a thing, if I had not seen it," is a common preface or appendix to a narrative of marvels ; and usually calls forth from an intelligent hearer, the appropriate answer, " *no more will I.*"

Let us however endeavour to trace up some of this hear-say evidence as far towards its source as we are able. Most persons would refer to the *newspapers* as the authority from which their knowledge on the subject was derived; so that, generally speaking, we may say, it is on the testimony of the newspapers that men believe in the existence and exploits of Napoleon Buonaparte.

It is rather a remarkable circumstance, that it is common to hear Englishmen speak of the impudent fabrications of foreign newspapers, and express wonder that any one can be found to credit them; while they conceive that, in this favoured land, the liberty of the press is a sufficient security for veracity. It is true they often speak contemptuously of such " newspaper stories" as last but a short time; indeed they continually see them contradicted within a day or two in the same paper, or their falsity detected by some journal of an opposite party; but still whatever is *long adhered to* and often *repeated,* especially if it also appear in *several different* papers, (and this, though they notoriously copy from one another) is almost sure to be generally believed. Whence this high respect which is practically paid to newspaper authority? Do men think that because a witness has been perpetually detected in falsehood, he may therefore be the more safely believed whenever he is *not* detected? or does adherence to a story, and frequent repetition of it, render it the more credible ? On the contrary, is it not a common remark in other cases, that a liar will generally stand to and reiterate what he has once said, merely because he *has* said it?

Let us if possible divest ourselves of this superstitious veneration for every thing that appears " in print," and examine a little more systematically the evidence which is adduced.

I suppose it will not be denied, that the three following are among the most important points to be ascertained, in deciding on the credibility of witnesses ; first, whether they have the means of gaining correct information; secondly, whether they have any interest in concealing truth, or propagating falsehood ; and, thirdly, whether they agree in their testimony. Let us examine the present witnesses upon all these points.

First, what means have the editors of newspapers for gaining correct information ? We know not, except from their own statements. Besides what is copied from other journals, foreign or British, (which is usually more than three-fourths of the news published,*) they

* " Suppose a fact to be transmitted through twenty per-
" sons; the first communicating it to the second, the second
" to the third, &c., and let the probability of each testimony
" be expressed by nine-tenths, (that is, suppose that of ten

profess to refer to the authority of certain
private correspondents abroad; *who* these correspondents are, what means *they* have of
obtaining information, or whether they exist at
all, we have no way of ascertaining. We find
ourselves in the condition of the Hindoos, who
are told by their priests, that the earth stands
on an elephant, and the elephant on a tortoise;
but are left to find out for themselves what the
tortoise stands on, or whether it stands on any
thing at all.

So much for our clear knowledge of the
means of *information* possessed by these wit-

" reports made by each witness, nine only are true,) then, at
" every time the story passes from one witness to another,
" the evidence is reduced to nine-tenths of what it was
" before.   Thus, after it has passed through the whole
" twenty, the evidence will be found to be less than one-
" eighth."   LA PLACE.   *Essai Philosophique sur les Pro-
babilités.*

That is, the chances for the fact thus attested being true,
will be, according to this distinguished calculator, less than
one in eight. Very few of the common newspaper-stories
however, relating to foreign countries, could be traced, if the
matter were carefully investigated, up to an actual eye-witness,
even through twenty intermediate witnesses ; and many of the
steps of our ladder would, I fear, prove but rotten ; few of
the reporters would deserve to have *one in ten* fixed as the
proportion of their false accounts.

nesses ; next, for the grounds on which we are to calculate on their *veracity.*

Have they not a manifest interest in circulating the wonderful accounts of Napoleon Buonaparte and his achievements, whether true or false ? Few would read newspapers if they did not sometimes find wonderful or important news in them ; and we may safely say that no subject was ever found so inexhaustibly interesting as the present.

It may be urged, however, that there are several adverse political parties of which the various public prints are respectively the organs, and who would not fail to expose each other's fabrications.* Doubtless they would, if they could do so without at the same time exposing *their own;* but identity of interests may induce a community of operations up to a certain point. And let it be observed, that the object of contention between these rival parties is, *who* shall have the administration of

* " I did not mention the difficulty of detecting a false-
" hood in any private or even public history, at the time and
" place where it is said to happen ; much more where the
" scene is removed to ever so small a distance. . . . .
" . . . . But the matter never comes to any
" issue, if trusted to the common method of altercation and
" debate and flying rumours." *Hume's Essay on Miracles,*
p. 195. 12mo; pp. 200, 201. 8vo. 1767; p. 127. 8vo. 1817.

B

public affairs, the control of public expenditure, and the disposal of places: the question, I say, is, not, whether the people shall be governed or not, but, *by which party* they shall be governed;—not whether the taxes shall be paid or not, but *who* shall *receive* them. Now it must be admitted, that Buonaparte is a political bugbear, most convenient to any administration: " if you do not adopt our measures " and reject those of our opponents, Buonaparte " will be sure to prevail over you; if you do " not submit to the Government, at least under " *our* administration, this formidable enemy will " take advantage of your insubordination, to " conquer and enslave you: pay your taxes " cheerfully, or the tremendous Buonaparte " will take all from you." Buonaparte, in short, was the burden of every song; his redoubted name was the charm which always succeeded in unloosing the purse-strings of the nation. And let us not be too sure, safe as we now think ourselves, that some occasion may not occur for again producing on the stage so useful a personage: it is not merely to naughty children in the nursery that the threat of being " given to Buonaparte" has proved effectual.

It is surely probable, therefore, that, with an object substantially the same, all parties may

have availed themselves of one common in-
strument. It is not necessary to suppose that
for this purpose they secretly entered into a formal agreement: though by the way, there are
reports afloat, that the editors of the *Courier*
and *Morning Chronicle* hold amicable consulta-
tions as to the conduct of their public warfare:
I will not take upon me to say that this is incredible; but at any rate it is not necessary for
the establishment of the probability I contend
for. Neither again would I imply that *all* news-
paper-editors are utterers of forged stories,
"knowing them to be forged;" most likely the
great majority of them publish what they find in
other papers with the same simplicity that their
readers peruse it; and therefore, it must be observed, are not at all more proper than their
readers to be cited as authorities.

Still it will be said, that unless we suppose
a regularly preconcerted plan, we must at least
expect to find great discrepancies in the accounts published. Though they might adopt
the general outline of facts one from another,
they would have to fill up the detail for themselves; and in this therefore we should meet
with infinite and irreconcileable variety.

Now this is precisely the point I am tending
to; for the fact exactly accords with the above

supposition; the discordance and mutual contradictions of these witnesses being such as
would alone throw a considerable shade of
doubt over their testimony. It is not in minute
circumstances alone that the discrepancy appears, such as might be expected to appear
in a narrative substantially true; but in very
great and leading transactions, and such as
are very intimately connected with the supposed hero. For instance, it is by no means
agreed whether Buonaparte led in person the
celebrated charge over the bridge of Lodi,
(for *celebrated* it certainly is, as well as the
siege of Troy, whether either event ever really
took place or no,) or was safe in the rear, while
Augereau performed the exploit.   The same
doubt hangs over the charge of the French
cavalry at Waterloo.   The peasant Lacoste, who
professed to have been Buonaparte's guide on
the day of the battle, and who earned a fortune
by detailing over and over again to visitors, all
the particulars of what the great man said and
did up to the moment of flight,—this same
Lacoste has been suspected by others, besides
me, of having never even been near the great
man, and having fabricated the whole story for
the sake of making a gain of the credulity of
travellers.   In the accounts that are extant of

the battle itself, published by persons professing
to have been present, the reader will find that
there is a discrepancy of *three or four hours* as
to the time when the battle began! A battle,
be it remembered, not fought with javelins and
arrows, like those of the ancients, in which one
part of a large army might be engaged, while a
distant portion of the same army knew nothing
of it; but a battle commencing (if indeed it
were ever fought at all) with the *firing of can-
non*, which would have announced pretty loudly
what was going on. It is no less uncertain
whether or no this strange personage poisoned
in Egypt an hospital-full of his own soldiers;
and butchered in cold blood a garrison that
had surrendered. But not to multiply instances; the battle of Borodino, which is represented as one of the greatest ever fought,
is unequivocally claimed as a victory by both
parties; nor is the question decided at this
day. We have official accounts on both sides,
circumstantially detailed, in the names of supposed respectable persons, professing to have
been present on the spot; yet totally irreconcileable. *Both* these accounts *may* be false;
but since *one* of them *must* be false, that one
(it is no matter *which* we suppose) proves in-
controvertibly this important maxim; that *it*

*is possible for a narrative—however circumstan-
tial—however steadily maintained—however public, and however important, the events it relates—
however grave the authority on which it is published—to be nevertheless an entire fabrication!*

Many of the events which have been recorded were probably believed much the more
readily and firmly, from the apparent caution
and hesitation with which they were at first
published,—the vehement contradiction in our
papers of many pretended French accounts,—
and the abuse lavished upon them for falsehood, exaggeration, and gasconade. But is it
not possible,—is it not indeed perfectly natural,—that the publishers even of known falsehood should assume this cautious demeanour,
and this abhorrence of exaggeration, in order
the more easily to gain credit? Is it not also
very possible, that those who actually believed
what they published, may have suspected mere
exaggeration in stories which were entire *fic-
tions?* Many men have that sort of simplicity,
that they think themselves quite secure against
being deceived, provided they believe only
part of the story they hear; when perhaps
the whole is equally false. So that perhaps
these simple-hearted editors, who were so vehement against lying bulletins, and so wary

in announcing their great news, were in the
condition of a clown, who thinks he has bought
a great bargain of a Jew, because he has beat
down the price perhaps from a guinea to a
crown, for some article that is not really worth
a groat.

With respect to the character of Buonaparte, the dissonance is if possible still greater.
According to some he was a wise, humane, magnanimous hero; others paint him as a monster
of cruelty, meanness, and perfidy : some, even
of those who are the most inveterate against
him, speak very highly of his political and
military ability; others place him on the very
verge of insanity. But allowing that all this
may be the colouring of party-prejudice, (which
surely is allowing a great deal,) there is one
point to which such a solution will hardly
apply : if there be any thing that can be clearly
ascertained in history, one would think it must
be the *personal courage* of a *military man ;*
yet here we are as much at a loss as ever ;
at the very same times and on the same occasions, he is described by different writers as a
man of undaunted intrepidity, and as an absolute
poltroon.

What then are we to believe ? if we are disposed to credit all that is told us, we must

believe in the existence not only of one, but of two or three Buonapartes; if we admit nothing but what is well authenticated, we shall be compelled to doubt of the existence of any.*

It appears, then, that those on whose testimony the existence and actions of Buonaparte are generally believed, fail in ALL the most essential points on which the credibility of witnesses depends: first, we have no assurance that they have access to correct information; secondly, they have an apparent interest in propagating falsehood; and, thirdly, they palpably contradict each other in the most important points.

Another circumstance which throws additional suspicion on these tales is, that the whig-party, as they are called, — the warm advocates for liberty, and opposers of the encroachments of monarchical power,—have for some time past strenuously espoused the cause, and vindicated the character of Buonaparte, who is represented by all as having been, if

---

* "We entertain a suspicion concerning any matter of "fact, when the witnesses *contradict* each other; when they "are of a *suspicious* character: when they have an *interest* "in what they affirm." *Hume's Essay on Miracles*, p. 172. 12mo; p. 176. 8vo. 1767; p. 113. 8vo. 1817.

not a tyrant, at least an absolute despot. One of the most forward in this cause is a gentleman, who once stood foremost in holding up this very man to public execration,—who first published, and long maintained against popular incredulity, the accounts of his atrocities in Egypt. Now that such a course should be adopted for party-purposes, by those who are aware that the whole story is a fiction, and the hero of it imaginary, seems not very incredible; but if they believed in the real existence of this despot, I cannot conceive how they could so forsake their principles as to advocate his cause, and eulogize his character.

After all, it may be expected that many who perceive the force of these objections, will yet be loth to think it possible that they and the public at large can have been so long and so greatly imposed upon. And thus it is that the magnitude and boldness of a fraud become its best support; the millions who for so many ages have believed in Mahomet or Brahma, lean as it were on each other for support; and not having vigour of mind enough boldly to throw off vulgar prejudices, and dare be wiser than the multitude, persuade themselves that what so many have acknowledged, must be true. But I call on those who boast their philosophical freedom of thought, and would fain tread in the steps of Hume and other inquirers of the like exalted and speculative genius, to follow up fairly and fully their own principles, and, throwing off the shackles of authority, to examine carefully the evidence of whatever is proposed to them, before they admit its truth.

That even in this enlightened age, as it is called, a whole nation may be egregiously imposed upon, even in matters which intimately concern them, may be proved (if it has not been already proved) by the following instance : it was stated in the newspapers, that, a month after the battle of Trafalgar, an English officer, who had been a prisoner of war, and was exchanged, returned to this country from France, and, beginning to condole with his countrymen on the terrible *defeat* they had sustained, was infinitely astonished to learn that the battle of Trafalgar was a splendid victory : he had been assured, he said, that in that battle the English had been totally defeated ; and the French were fully and universally persuaded that such was the fact. Now if this report of the belief of the French nation was *not* true, the British Public were completely imposed upon ; if it *were* true, then both nations were, at the same time, rejoicing in the event of the same battle, as a signal victory to themselves ; and consequently one or other, at least, of these nations must have been the dupes of their Government : for if the battle was never fought at all, or was not decisive on either side, in that case *both* parties were deceived. This instance, I conceive, is absolutely demonstrative of the point in question.

" But what shall we say to the testimony of " those many respectable persons who went to " Plymouth on purpose, and saw Buonaparte " with their own eyes? must they not trust " their senses ?" I would not disparage either the eye-sight or the veracity of these gentlemen. I am ready to allow that they went to Plymouth for the purpose of seeing Buonaparte ; nay more, that they actually rowed out into the harbour in a boat, and came alongside of a man-of-war, on whose deck they saw a man in a cocked hat, who, *they were told*, was Buonaparte. This is the utmost point to which their testimony goes; how they ascertained that this man in the cocked hat had gone through all the marvellous and romantic adventures with which we have so long been amused, we are not told. Did they perceive in his physiognomy, his true name, and authentic

history? Truly this evidence is such as country-
people give one for a story of apparitions; if
you discover any signs of incredulity, they
triumphantly shew the very house which the
ghost haunted, the identical dark corner where
it used to vanish, and perhaps even the tomb-
stone of the person whose death it foretold.
Jack Cade's nobility was supported by the
same irresistible kind of evidence: having
asserted that the eldest son of Edmund Mor-
timer, Earl of March, was stolen by a beggar-
woman, " became a bricklayer when he came
" to age," and was the father of the supposed
Jack Cade: one of his companions confirms
the story, by saying, " Sir, he made a chimney
" in my father's house, and the bricks are
" alive at this day to testify it; therefore deny
" it not."

Much of the same kind is the testimony of
our brave countrymen, who are ready to produce the scars they received in fighting against
this terrible Buonaparte. That they fought
and were wounded, they may safely testify;
and probably they no less firmly *believe* what
they were *told* respecting the cause in which
they fought: it would have been a high breach
of discipline to doubt it; and they, I conceive,
are men better skilled in handling a musket,

than in sifting evidence, and detecting imposture. But I defy any one of them to come
forward and declare, *on his own knowledge,*
what was the cause in which he fought,—
under whose commands the opposed generals
acted,—and whether the person who issued
those commands did really perform the mighty
achievements we are told of.

Let those then who pretend to philosophical
freedom of inquiry,—who scorn to rest their
opinions on popular belief, and to shelter themselves under the example of the unthinking
multitude, consider carefully each one for himself, what is the evidence proposed to himself in
particular, for the existence of such a person as
Napoleon Buonaparte : (I do not mean whether
there ever was a person bearing that *name,* for
that is a question of no consequence, but whether any such person ever performed all the wonderful things attributed to him) ; let him then
weigh well the objections to that evidence, (of
which I have given but a hasty and imperfect
sketch,) and if he then finds it amount to any
thing *more* than a probability, I have only to
congratulate him on his easy faith.

But the same testimony which would have
great weight in establishing a thing intrinsically
probable, will lose part of this weight in pro-

portion as the matter attested is improbable;
and if adduced in support of any thing that is
at variance with uniform experience,* will be
rejected at once by all sound reasoners. Let
us then consider what sort of a story it is that
is proposed to our acceptance. How grossly
contradictory are the reports of the different
authorities, I have already remarked: but consider, by itself, the story told by any one of
them; it carries an air of fiction and romance on
the very face of it; all the events are great, and
splendid, and marvellous;† great armies, great
victories, great frosts, great reverses, " hair-
" breadth 'scapes," empires subverted in a few
days; every thing happening in defiance of

* " That testimony itself derives all its force from expe-
" rience, seems very certain. . . . .
" . . . The first author, we believe, who stated fairly
" the connexion between the evidence of testimony and
" the evidence of experience, was HUME, in his Essay on
" Miracles, a work . . . abounding in maxims of great use
" in the conduct of life." *Edinb. Review*, Sept. 1814, p. 328.

† " Suppose, for instance, that the fact which the testimony
" endeavours to establish partakes of the extraordinary and
" the marvellous; in that case, the evidence resulting from
" the testimony receives a diminution, greater or less in
" proportion as the fact is more or less unusual." *Hume's
Essay on Miracles*, p. 173. 12mo; p. 176. 8vo. 1767 ; p. 113.
8vo. 1817.

political calculations, and in opposition to the *experience* of past times ; every thing upon that grand scale, so common in Epic Poetry, so rare in real life ; and thus calculated to strike the imagination of the vulgar,—and to remind the sober-thinking few of the Arabian Nights. Every event too has that *roundness* and completeness which is so characteristic of fiction ; nothing is done by halves ; we have *complete* victories,— *total* overthrows,—*entire* subversion of empires, —*perfect* reestablishments of them,—crowded upon us in rapid succession. To enumerate the improbabilities of each of the several parts of this history, would fill volumes ; but they are so fresh in every one's memory, that there is no need of such a detail : let any judicious man, not ignorant of history and of human nature, revolve them in his mind, and consider how far they are conformable to Experience,* our best and only sure guide. In vain will he seek in history for something similar to this wonderful Buonaparte ; " nought but himself can be his parallel."

* " The ultimate standard by which we determine all dis-
" putes that may arise is always derived from experience and
" observation." *Hume's Essay on Miracles,* p. 172. 12mo ;
p. 175. 8vo. 1767 ; p. 112. 8vo. 1817.

Will the conquests of Alexander be compared
with his? *They* were effected over a rabble of
effeminate undisciplined barbarians; else his
progress would hardly have been so rapid:
witness his father Philip, who was much longer
occupied in subduing the comparatively insig-
nificant territory of the warlike and civilized
Greeks, notwithstanding their being divided into
numerous petty states, whose mutual jealousy
enabled him to contend with them separately.
But the Greeks had never made such progress in
arts and arms as the great and powerful states
of Europe, which Buonaparte is represented as
so speedily overpowering. His empire has been
compared to the Roman : mark the contrast;
he gains in a few years, that dominion, or at
least control, over Germany, wealthy, civilized,
and powerful, which the Romans in the plenitude
of their power could not obtain, during a struggle
of as many centuries, against the ignorant half-
savages who then possessed it ?

Another peculiar circumstance in the history
of this extraordinary personage is, that when
it is found convenient to represent him as defeated, though he is by no means defeated by
halves, but involved in much more sudden and
total ruin than the personages of real history

usually meet with; yet, if it is thought fit he
should be restored, it is done as quickly and
completely as if Merlin's rod had been employed. He enters Russia with a prodigious
army, which is totally ruined by an unprecedented hard winter; (every thing relating to
this man is *prodigious* and *unprecedented;*) yet
in a few months we find him intrusted with
another great army in Germany, which is also
totally ruined at Leipsic; making, inclusive of
the Egyptian, the third great army thus totally
lost: yet the French are so good-natured as
to furnish him with another, sufficient to make
a formidable stand in France; he is however
conquered, and presented with the sovereignty of
Elba; (surely, by the bye, some more *probable*
way might have been found of disposing of
him, till again wanted, than to place him thus
on the very verge of his ancient dominions;)
thence he returns to France, where he is received with open arms, and enabled to lose a
fifth great army at Waterloo: yet so eager
were these people to be a sixth time led to
destruction, that it was found necessary to
confine *him* in an island some thousand miles
off, and to quarter foreign troops upon *them,*
lest they should make an insurrection in his

c

favour!* Does any one believe all this, and
yet refuse to believe a miracle? Or rather,
what is this but a miracle? Is it not a
violation of the laws of nature? for surely there
are moral laws of nature as well as physical;
which though more liable to exceptions in this
or that particular case, are no less *true as
general rules* than the laws of matter, and
therefore cannot be violated and contradicted
beyond a certain point, without a miracle.†

* ᾽Η θαύματα πολλά.

Καὶ πού τι καὶ βροτῶν φρένας

ΎΠΕΡ ΤΟΝ ΑΛΗΘΗ ΛΟΓΟΝ

Λεδαιδαλμένοι ψεύδεσι ποικίλοις

᾽Εξαπατῶντι μῦθοι.   PIND. Olymp. 1.

† This doctrine, though hardly needing confirmation from
authority, is supported by that of Hume : his eighth essay is,
throughout, an argument for the doctrine of Philosophical
" necessity," drawn entirely from the general uniformity
observable in the course of nature with respect to the principles of *human conduct*, as well as those of the material uni-
verse ; from which uniformity, he observes, it is that we
are enabled, *in both cases*, to form our judgments by means
of *Experience :* " and if," says he, " we would explode any
" forgery in history, we cannot make use of a more convin-
" cing argument, than to prove that the actions ascribed to
" any person, are directly contrary to the course of nature .
" . . . . The veracity of
" Quintus Curtius is as suspicious when he describes the
" supernatural courage of Alexander, by which he was hur-

Nay, there is this additional circumstance which renders the contradiction of Experience

" ried on single to attack multitudes, as when he describes
" his supernatural force and activity, by which he was able
" to resist them. So readily and universally do we acknow-
" ledge a *uniformity in human motives and actions as well as*
" *in the operations of body.*" *Eighth Essay*, p. 131. 12mo ;
p. 85. 8vo. 1817.

Accordingly, in the tenth essay, his use of the term " mira-
" cle," after having called it " a transgression of a law of
" nature," plainly shews that he meant to include *human*
nature : " no testimony," says he, " is sufficient to establish
" a miracle, unless the testimony be of such a nature that its
" falsehood would be more miraculous than the fact which it
" endeavours to establish :" the term " prodigy" also (which
he all along employs as synonymous with " miracle " is applied to testimony, in the same manner, immediately after:
" In the foregoing reasoning we have supposed . . . . .
" that the falsehood of that testimony would be a kind of
" prodigy." Now had he meant to confine the meaning of
" miracle," and " prodigy," to a violation of the laws of
matter, the epithet " *miraculous*," applied even thus hypo-
thetically, to *false testimony*, would be as unmeaning as the
epithets " green," or " square ;" the only possible sense in
which we can apply to it, even in imagination, the term
" miraculous," is that of " highly improbable,"—" contrary
" to those laws of nature which respect human conduct :" and
in this sense accordingly he uses the word in the very next
sentence : " When any one tells me that he saw a dead man
" restored to life, I immediately consider with myself whether
" it be more *probable* that this person should either deceive
" or be deceived, or that the fact which he relates should

more glaring in this case than in that of the
miraculous histories which ingenious sceptics
have held up to contempt: all the advocates
of miracles admit that they are rare exceptions
to the general course of nature ; but contend
that they must needs be so, on account of the
rarity of those extraordinary *occasions* which
are the *reason* of their being performed : a
Miracle, they say, does not happen every day,
because a Revelation is not given every day.
It would be foreign to the present purpose
to seek for arguments against this answer ;
I leave it to those who are engaged in the
controversy, to find a reply to it ; but my present object is, to point out that this solution
does not at all apply in the present case.
Where is the peculiarity of the *occasion ?*　What

" really have happened. I weigh the one *miracle* against
" the other." *Hume's Essay on Miracles,* p. 176, 177. 12mo ;
p. 182. 8vo. 1767 ; p. 115. 8vo. 1817.

See also a passage above quoted from the same essay,
where he speaks of " the *miraculous* accounts of travellers ;"
evidently using the word in this sense. Perhaps it was su-
perfluous to cite authority for applying the term " miracle"
to whatever is highly "improbable ;" but it is important to
the students of Hume, to be fully aware that *he* uses those
two expressions as synonymous; since otherwise they would
mistake the meaning of that passage which he justly calls
" a general maxim worthy of our attention."

sufficient *reason* is there for a series of events occurring in the eighteenth and nineteenth centuries, which never took place before? Was Europe at that period peculiarly weak, and in a state of barbarism, that one man could achieve such conquests, and acquire such a vast empire? On the contrary, she was flourishing in the height of strength and civilization. Can the persevering attachment and blind devotedness of the French to this man, be accounted for by his being the descendant of a long line of kings, whose race was hallowed by hereditary veneration? No; we are told he was a low-born usurper, and not even a Frenchman! Is it that he was a good and kind sovereign? he is represented not only as an imperious and merciless despot, but as most wantonly careless of the lives of his soldiers. Could the French army and people have failed to hear from the wretched survivors of his supposed Russian expedition, how they had left the corpses of above 100,000 of their comrades bleaching on the snow-drifts of that dismal country, whither his mad ambition had conducted them, and where his selfish cowardice had deserted them? Wherever we turn to seek for circumstances that may help to account for the events of this incredible story, we only meet with such as aggra-

vate its improbability.*   Had it been told of
some distant country, at a remote period, we
could not have told what peculiar circumstances there might have been to render probable what seems to us most strange; and yet
in *that* case every philosophical sceptic; every
free-thinking speculator, would instantly have
rejected such a history, as utterly unworthy of
credit.   What, for instance, would the great
Hume, or any of the philosophers of his school
have said, if they had found in the antique
records of any nation such a passage as this:
" There was a certain man of Corsica, whose
" name was Napoleon, and he was one of the
" chief captains of the host of the French;
" and he gathered together an army, and went
" and fought against Egypt: but when the
" king of Britain heard thereof, he sent ships
" of war and valiant men to fight against the
" French in Egypt. So they warred against
" them, and prevailed, and strengthened the

* " Events may be so extraordinary that they can hardly
" be established by testimony. We would not give credit
" to a man who would affirm that he saw an hundred dice
" thrown in the air, and that they all fell on the same faces."
Edinb. Review, Sept. 1814, p. 327.
Let it be observed, that the instance here given is *miraculous* in no other sense but that of being highly *improbable*.

" hands of the rulers of the land against the
" French, and drave away Napoleon from be-
" fore the city of Acre. Then Napoleon left
" the captains and the army that were in
" Egypt, and fled, and returned back to
" France. So the French people took Na-
" poleon, and made him ruler over them, and
" he became exceeding great, insomuch that
" there was none like him of all that had ruled
" over France before."

What, I say, would Hume have thought of
this, especially if he had been told that it was
at this day generally credited? Would he not
have confessed that he had been mistaken in
supposing there was a peculiarly blind credulity and prejudice in favour of every thing that
is accounted *sacred;* * for that, since even
professed sceptics swallow implicitly such a
story as this, it appears there must be a still
blinder prejudice in favour of every thing that
is *not* accounted sacred ?

Suppose, again, we found in this history such
passages as the following: " And it came

* " If the spirit of religion join itself to the love of wonder,
" there is an end of common sense ; and human testimony in
" these circumstances loses all pretensions to authority."
Hume's Essay on Miracles, p. 179. 12mo ; p. 185. 8vo. 1767 ;
p. 117. 8vo. 1817.

" to pass after these things that Napoleon
" strengthened himself, and gathered together
" another host instead of that which he had
" lost, and went and warred against the Prus-
" sians, and the Russians, and the Austrians,
" and all the rulers of the north country,
" which were confederate against him.   And
" the ruler of Sweden also, which was a
" Frenchman, warred against Napoleon.   So
" they went forth, and fought against the
" French in the plain of Leipsic.   And the
" French were discomfited before their enemies,
" and fled and came to the rivers which are
" behind Leipsic, and essayed to pass over,
" that they might escape out of the hand
" of their enemies; but they could not; for
" Napoleon had broken down the bridges; so
" the people of the north countries came upon
" them, and smote them with a very grievous
" slaughter."   .   .   .   .
        .   .   .   .   .

    " Then the ruler of Austria and all the
" rulers of the north countries sent messengers
" unto Napoleon to speak peaceably unto him,
" saying, Why should there be war between
" us any more?   Now Napoleon had put
" away his wife, and taken the daughter of
" the ruler of Austria to wife.   So all the

" counsellors of Napoleon came and stood
" before him, and said, Behold now these
" kings are merciful kings; do even as they
" say unto thee; knowest thou not yet that
" France is destroyed? But he spake roughly
" unto his counsellors, and drave them out
" from his presence, neither would he hearken
" unto their voice. And when all the kings
" saw that they warred against France, and
" smote it with the edge of the sword, and
" came near to Paris, which is the royal city,
" to take it: so the men of Paris went out,
" and delivered up the city to them. Then
" those kings spake kindly unto the men of
" Paris, saying, Be of good cheer, there shall
" no harm happen unto you. Then were the
" men of Paris glad, and said, Napoleon is a
" tyrant; he shall no more rule over us: also
" all the princes, the judges, the counsellors,
" and the captains whom Napoleon had raised
" up even from the lowest of the people, sent
" unto Lewis the brother of King Lewis, whom
" they had slain, and made him king over
" France." . . . .
. . . . . .

" And when Napoleon saw that the king-
" dom was departed from him, he said unto
" the rulers which came against him, Let me,

" I pray you, give the kingdom unto my son:
" but they would not hearken unto him. Then
" he spake yet again, saying, Let me, I pray
" you, go and live in the island of Elba, which
" is over against Italy, nigh unto the coast of
" France; and ye shall give me an allowance
" for me and my household, and the land of
" Elba also for a possession. So they made
" him ruler of Elba." . . . .

. . . .

. . . .

" In those days the Pope returned unto
" his own land. Now the French, and divers
" other nations of Europe, are servants of the
" Pope, and hold him in reverence; but he is
" an abomination unto the Britons, and to the
" Prussians, and to the Russians, and to the
" Swedes. Howbeit the French had taken
" away all his lands, and robbed him of all
" that he had, and carried him away captive
" into France. But when the Britons and
" the Prussians, and the Russians, and the
" Swedes, and the rest of the nations that were
" confederate against France, came thither,
" they caused the French to set the Pope at
" liberty, and to restore all his goods that they
" had taken; likewise they gave him back all
" his possessions; and he went home in peace,

" and ruled over his own city as in times past."

. . . .

. . . .

" And it came to pass when Napoleon had
" not yet been a full year at Elba, that he
" said unto his men of war which clave unto
" him, Go to, let us go back to France, and
" fight against King Lewis, and thrust him
" out from being king. So he departed, he
" and six hundred men with him that drew the
" sword, and warred against King Lewis. Then
" all the men of Belial gathered themselves
" together, and said, God save Napoleon. And
" when Lewis saw that he fled, and gat him
" into the land of Batavia : and Napoleon ruled
" over France," &c. &c. &c.

Now if a freethinking philosopher—one of
those who advocate the cause of unbiassed
reason, and despised pretended revelations—
were to meet with such a tissue of absurdities
as this, in an old Jewish record, would he not
reject it at once as too palpable an imposture*

* " I desire any one to lay his hand upon his heart, and
" after serious consideration declare whether he thinks that
" the falsehood of such a book, supported by such testimony,
" would be more extraordinary and miraculous than all the
" miracles it relates." *Hume's Essay on Miracles*, p. 200.
12mo ; p. 206. 8vo. 1767 ; p. 131. 8vo. 1817.

to deserve even any inquiry into its evidence?
Is that credible then of the civilized Europeans
now, which could not, if reported of the semi-
barbarous Jews 3000 years ago, be established
by any testimony? Will it be answered, that
"there is nothing *supernatural* in all this?"
Why is it, then, that you object to what is
supernatural—that you reject every account of
miracles—if not because they are *improbable?*
Surely then a story equally or still more
improbable, is not to be implicitly received,
merely on the ground that it is *not* miraculous:
though in fact, as I have already (in note p. 34.)
shewn from Hume's authority, it really *is* miraculous. The opposition to Experience has
been proved to be as complete in this case, as
in what are commonly called miracles; and
the reasons assigned for that contrariety by the
defenders of *them,* cannot be pleaded in the
present instance. If then philosophers, who
reject every wonderful story that is maintained
by priests, are yet found ready to believe *every
thing else,* however improbable, they will surely
lay themselves open to the accusation brought

Let it be borne in mind, that Hume (as I have above
remarked) continually employs the terms "miracle" and
" prodigy" to signify any thing that is highly *improbable* and
extraordinary.

against them of being unduly prejudiced against whatever relates to religion.

There is one more circumstance which I cannot forbear mentioning, because it so much adds to the air of fiction which pervades every part of this marvellous tale ; and that is, the *nationality* of it.*

Buonaparte prevailed over all the hostile states in turn, *except England;* in the zenith of his power, his fleets were swept from the sea, *by England;* his troops always defeat an equal, and frequently even a superior number of those of any other nation, *except the English;* and with them it is just the reverse ; twice, and twice only, he is personally engaged against an *English commander,* and both times he is totally defeated ; at Acre and at Waterloo ; and to crown all, *England* finally crushes this tremendous power, which has so long kept the continent in subjection or in alarm, and to the *English* he surrenders himself prisoner ! Thoroughly national to be sure ! It *may* be all very true ; but I would only ask, *if* a story *had*

* " The wise lend a very academic faith to every report " which favours the passion of the reporter, whether it mag- " nifies his *country,* his family, or himself." *Hume's Essay on Miracles,* p. 144. 12mo ; p. 200. 8vo. 1767 ; p. 126. 8vo. 1817.

been fabricated for the express purpose of amusing the English nation, could it have been contrived more ingeniously? It would do admirably for an epic poem; and indeed bears a considerable resemblance to the Iliad and the Æneid; in which Achilles and the Greeks, Æneas and the Trojans, (the ancestors of the Romans,) are so studiously held up to admiration. Buonaparte's exploits seem magnified in order to enhance the glory of his conquerors; just as Hector is allowed to triumph during the absence of Achilles, merely to give additional splendour to his overthrow by the arm of that invincible hero. Would not this circumstance alone render a history rather *suspicious* in the eyes of an acute critic, even if it were not filled with such gross improbabilities; and induce him to suspend his judgment, till very satisfactory evidence (far stronger than can be found in this case) should be produced.

Is it then too much to demand of the wary academic * a suspension of judgment as to the " life and adventures of Napoleon Buonaparte?"

---

* " Nothing can be more contrary than such a philosophy " (the academic or sceptical) "to the supine indolence of the " mind, its rash arrogance, its lofty pretensions, and its " superstitious credulity." *Fifth Essay*, p. 68. 12mo; p. 41. 8vo. 1817.

I do not pretend to *decide* positively that there is not, nor ever was, any such person; but merely to propose it as a *doubtful* point, and one the more deserving of careful investigation, from the very circumstance of its having hitherto been admitted without inquiry. Far less would I undertake to decide what is, or has been, the real state of affairs: he who points out the improbability of the current story, is not bound to suggest an hypothesis of his own;* though it may safely be affirmed, that it would be hard to invent any, more improbable than the received one. One may surely be allowed to hesitate in admitting the stories which the ancient poets tell, of earthquakes and volcanic eruptions being caused by imprisoned giants, without being called upon satisfactorily to account for those phenomena.

Amidst the defect of valid evidence under which, as I have already shewn, we labour in the present instance, it is hardly possible to offer more than here and there a probable conjecture; or to pronounce how much may be true, and how much fictitious, in the accounts presented to us. For it is to be observed that

* See Hume's Essay on Miracles, p. 189, 191, 195. 12mo; p. 193, 197, 201, 202. 8vo. 1767; p. 124, 125, 126. 8vo. 1817.

this case is much *more* open to sceptical doubts
even than some miraculous histories ; for some
of them are of such a nature that you cannot
consistently admit a part and reject the rest ;
but are bound, if you are satisfied as to the
reality of any one miracle, to embrace the
whole system ; so that it is necessary for the
sceptic to impeach the evidence of *all* of them,
separately, and collectively : whereas *here*
each single point requires to be *established*
separately, since no one of them authenticates
the rest. Supposing there be a state-prisoner
at St. Helena, (which, by the way, it is acknowledged many of the French disbelieve,)
how do we know who he is, or why he is
confined there ? There have been state-prisoners
before now, who were never guilty of sub-
jugating half Europe, and whose offences have
been very imperfectly ascertained. Admitting
that there have been bloody wars going on for
several years past, which is highly probable,
it does not follow that the events of those
wars were such as we have been told ;—that
Buonaparte was the author and conductor of
them ;—or that such a person ever existed.
What disturbances may have taken place in
the government of the French people, we, and
even nineteen-twentieths of *them*, have no means

of learning but from imperfect hear-say evidence: but that there have been numerous bloody wars with France under the dominion of the *Bourbons*, we are well assured : and we are now told that France is governed by a Bourbon king, of the name of Lewis, who professes to be in the twenty-third year of his reign. Let every one conjecture for himself. I am far from pretending to decide who may have been the governor or governors of the French nation, and the leaders of their armies, for several years past. Certain it is, that when men are indulging their inclination for the marvellous, they always shew a strong propensity to accumulate upon one individual (real or imaginary) the exploits of many ; besides multiplying and exaggerating these exploits a thousand-fold. Thus, the expounders of the ancient mythology tell us there were several persons of the name of Hercules, (either originally bearing that appellation, or having it applied to them as an honour,) whose collective feats, after being dressed up in a sufficiently marvellous garb, were attributed to a single hero. Is it not just possible, that during the rage for words of Greek derivation, the title of " Napoleon " (Ναπολεων), which signifies " Lion " of the forest," may have been conferred by the popular voice on more than one favourite

D

general, distinguished for irresistible valour?
Is it not also possible that " Buona parte" may
have been originally a sort of cant term applied
to the "good (i. e. the bravest or most patriotic)
"part" of the French army, collectively ; and
have been afterwards mistaken for the proper
name of an individual? I do not profess to support this conjecture ; but it is certain that such
mistakes may and do occur.   Some critics have
supposed that the Athenians imagined Anas-
tasis ("Resurrection") to be a new goddess,
in whose cause Paul was preaching.   Would
it have been thought anything incredible if
we had been told that the ancient Persians,
who had no idea of any but a monarchical government, had supposed Aristocratia to be a queen of
Sparta? but we need not confine ourselves to
hypothetical cases ; it is positively stated that
the Hindoos at this day believe " the honourable East India Company" to be a venerable
old Lady of high dignity, residing in this country.
The Germans of the present day derive their
name from a similar mistake ; the first tribe of
them who invaded Gaul* assumed the honour-

* Germaniæ vocabulum recens et nuper additum; quo-
niam, qui primi Rhenum transgressi Gallos expulerint, ac
nunc Tungri, tunc Germani vocati sint : ita nationis nomen
in nomen gentis evaluisse paullatim, ut omnes, primum a

able title of " *Ger-man*," which signifies " warrior ;" (the words, " war" and " guerre," as well
as " man," which remains in our language unal-
tered, are evidently derived from the Teutonic),
and the Gauls applied this as a *name* to the whole
race.

However, I merely throw out these conjec-
tures without by any means contending that
more plausible ones might not be suggested.
But whatever supposition we adopt, or whether
we adopt any, the objections to the commonly
received accounts will remain in their full force,
and imperiously demand the attention of the
candid sceptic.

I call upon those therefore who profess themselves advocates of free inquiry—who disdain
to be carried along with the stream of popular
opinion,—and who will listen to no testimony
that runs counter to experience,—to follow up
their own principles fairly and consistently.
Let the same mode of argument be adopted
in all cases alike; and then it can no longer
be attributed to hostile prejudice, but to enlarged and philosophical views. If they have
already rejected some histories, on the ground
of their being strange and marvellous,—of their

victore ob metum, mox a seipsis invento nomine, Germani
vocarentur. *Tacitus, de Mor. Germ.*

relating facts, unprecedented, and at variance
with the established course of nature,—let them
not give credit to another history which lies
open to the very same objections,—the extraordinary and romantic tale we have been just
considering. If they have discredited the testimony of witnesses, who are *said* at least to
have been disinterested, and to have braved
persecutions and death in support of their as-
sertions,—can these philosophers consistently
listen to and believe the testimony of those who
avowedly *get money* by the tales they publish,
and who do not even pretend that they incur any
serious risk in case of being detected in a falsehood ? If in other cases they have refused to
listen to an account which has passed through
many intermediate hands before it reaches them,
and which is defended by those who have an
interest in maintaining it; let them consider
through how many, and what very suspicious
hands, *this* story has arrived to them, without
the possibility (as I have shewn) of tracing it
back to any decidedly authentic source, after
all;* and likewise how strong an interest, in
every way, those who have hitherto imposed

---

* For let it not be forgotten, that these writers, *themselves,*
refer to no better authority than that of an *un-named and*
unknown foreign correspondent.

on them, have, in keeping up the imposture. Let them, in short, shew themselves as ready to detect the cheats, and despise the fables, of politicians, as of priests.

But if they are still wedded to the popular belief in this point, let them be consistent enough to admit the same evidence in *other* cases, which they yield to, in *this*. If after all that has been said, they cannot bring themselves to doubt of the existence of Napoleon Buonaparte, they must at least acknowledge that they do not apply to that question, the same plan of reasoning which they have made use of in others; and they are consequently bound in reason and in honesty to renounce it altogether.

POSTSCRIPT
TO THE THIRD EDITION.

It may seem arrogant for an obscure and nameless individual to claim the glory of having put to death the most formidable of all recorded heroes. But a shadowy champion may be overthrown by a shadowy antagonist. Many a terrific spectre has been laid by the beams of a halfpenny candle. And if I have succeeded in making out, in the foregoing pages, a probable case of suspicion, it must, I think, be admitted, that there is some ground for my present boast, of having *killed* Napoleon Buonaparte.

Let but the circumstances of the case be considered. This mighty Emperor, who had been so long the bugbear of the civilized world, after having obtained successes and undergone reverses, such as never befell any (other at least) *real* potentate, was at length sentenced to confinement in the remote island of St. Helena: a measure which many persons wondered at, and many objected to, on various grounds; not unreasonably supposing the illustrious exile to be a real person: but on the supposition of his being only a man of straw, the situation was exceedingly favorable for keeping him out of the way of impertinent curiosity, when not wanted, and for making him the foundation of any new plots that there might be occasion to conjure up.

About this juncture it was that the public attention
was first invited by these pages, to the question as to
the real existence of Napolean Buonaparte. They excited, it may be fairly supposed, along with much
surprise and much censure, some degree of doubt,
and probably of consequent inquiry. No fresh evidence, as far as I can learn, of the truth of the disputed points, was brought forward to dispel these
doubts. We heard, however, of the most jealous pre-
cautions being used to prevent any intercourse between the formidable prisoner, and any stranger,
who, from motives of curiosity, might wish to visit
him. The "man in the iron mask" could hardly have
been more rigorously secluded: and we also heard
various contradictory reports of conversations between him and the few who were allowed access to
him; the falsehood and inconsistency of most of these
reports being proved in contemporary publications.

At length, just about the time when the public
scepticism respecting this extraordinary personage
might be supposed to have risen to an alarming
height, it was announced to us that he was dead! A
stop was thus put, most opportunely, to all troublesome inquiries. I do not undertake to deny that such a
person did live and die. That he was, and that he did,
everything that is reported, we cannot believe, unless
we consent to admit contradictory statements; but
many of the events recorded, however marvellous, are
certainly not, when taken separately, physically impossible. But I would only entreat the candid reader
to reflect what might naturally be expected, on the
supposition of the surmises contained in the present
work being well founded. Supposing the whole of the

tale I have been considering to have been a fabrication, what would be the natural result of such an attempt to excite inquiry into its truth? Evidently the shortest and most effectual mode of eluding detection, would be to *kill* the phantom, and so get rid of him at once. A ready and decisive answer would thus be provided to any one in whom the foregoing arguments might have excited suspicions: "Sir, there can be no doubt that such a person existed, and performed what is related of him; and if you will just take a voyage to St. Helena, you may see with your own eyes,—not him indeed, for he is no longer living,—but his *tomb*: and what evidence would you have that is more decisive?"

So much for his *Death*: as for his *Life*,—it is just published by an eminent writer: besides which, the shops will supply us with abundance of busts and prints of this great man; all striking likenesses—of one another. The most incredulous must be satisfied with this!   "Stat magni NOMINIS umbra!"

KONX OMPAX.

POSTSCRIPT
TO THE SEVENTH EDITION.

Since the publication of the Sixth Edition of this work, the French nation, and the world at large, have obtained an additional evidence, to which I hope they will attach as much weight as it deserves, of the reality of the wonderful history I have been treating of. The Great Nation, among the many indications lately given of an heroic zeal like what Homer attributes to his Argive warriors, τίσασθαι ἙΛΕ΄ΝΗΣ ὁομήματά τε στοναχάς τε, have formed and executed the design of bringing home for honorable interment the remains of their illustrious Chief.

How many persons have actually inspected these relics, I have not ascertained; but that a real coffin, containing real bones, was brought from St. Helena to France, I see no reason to disbelieve.

Whether future visitors to St. Helena will be shown merely the identical *place* in which Buonaparte was (*said* to have been) interred, or whether another set of real bones will be exhibited in that island, we have yet to learn.

This latter supposition is not very improbable. It was something of a credit to the island, an attraction to strangers, and a source of profit to some of the inhabitants, to possess so remarkable a relic; and this glory and advantage they must naturally wish to retain. If so, there seems no reason why they should not have a Buonaparte of their own; for there is, I believe, no doubt that there are, or were, several Museums in England, which, among other curiosities, boasted, each, of a genuine skull of Oliver Cromwell.

Perhaps, therefore, we shall hear of several well-authenticated skulls of Buonaparte also, in the collections of different virtuosos, all of whom (especially those in whose own crania the "organ of wonder" is the most largely developed,) will doubtless derive equal satisfaction from the relics they respectively possess.

POSTSCRIPT
TO THE NINTH EDITION.

The Public has been of late much interested and not a little bewildered, by the accounts of many strange events, said to have recently taken place in France and other parts of the Continent. Are these accounts of such a character as to allay, or to strengthen and increase, such doubts as have been suggested in the foregoing pages?

We are told that there is now a Napoleon Buonaparte at the head of the government of France. It is not, indeed, asserted that he is the very original Napoleon Buonaparte himself. The death of that personage, and the transportation of his genuine bones to France, had been too widely proclaimed to allow of his reappearance in his own proper person. But "uno avulso, non deficit alter." Like the Thibetian worshippers of the Delai Lama, (who never dies; only, his soul transmigrates into a fresh body,) the French are so resolved, we are told, to be under a Buonaparte—whether that be a man or "a system"— that they have found, it seems, a kind of new incarnation of this their grand Lama, in a person said to be the nephew of the original one.

And when, on hearing that this personage now fills the high office of President of the French Republic, we inquire (very naturally) *how he came there*, we are informed that, several years ago, he invaded France in an English vessel, (the *English* having always been suspected of keeping Buonaparte ready, like the winds in a Lapland witch's bag, to be let out on occasion,) at the head of a force, not of six hundred men, like his supposed uncle in his expedition from Elba, but of fifty-five, (!) with which he landed at Boulogne, proclaimed himself emperor, and was joined by no less than *one* man! He was accordingly, we are told, arrested, brought to trial, and sentenced to imprisonment; but having, some years after, escaped from prison, and taken refuge in England, (*England* again!) he thence returned to France: and so the French nation placed him at the head of the government!

All this will doubtless be received as a very probable tale by those who have given full credit to all the stories I have alluded to in the foregoing pages.

POSTSCRIPT
TO THE ELEVENTH EDITION.

When any dramatic piece *takes*—as the phrase is—with the public, it will usually be represented again and again with still-continued applause; and sometimes imitations of it will be produced; so that the same drama in substance will, with occasional slight variations in the plot, and changes of names, long keep possession of the stage.

Something like this has taken place with respect to that curious tragi-comedy—the scene of it laid in France—which has engaged the attention of the British public for about sixty years; during which it has been "exhibited to crowded houses"—viz., coffee-houses, reading-rooms, &c., with unabated interest.

The outline of this drama, or series of dramas, may be thus sketched:

Dramatis Personæ

A.   A King or other Sovereign.
B.   His Queen.
C.   The Heir apparent.
D.E.F.   His Ministers.
G.H.I.J.K.   Demagogues.

L.

A popular leader of superior ingenuity, who becomes ultimately supreme ruler, under the title of Dictator, Consul, Emperor, King, President, or some other. Soldiers, Senators, Executioners, and other functionaries, Citizens, Fishwomen, &c.

Scene, Paris.

(1.)

The first Act of one of these dramas represents a monarchy, somewhat troubled by murmurs of disaffection, suspicions of conspiracy, &c.

(2.)

Second Act, a rebellion; in which ultimately the government is overthrown.

(3.)

Act the third, a provisional government established, on principles of liberty, equality, fraternity, &c.

(4.)

Act the fourth, struggles of various parties for power, carried on with sundry intrigues, and sanguinary conflicts.

(5.)

Act the fifth, the re-establishment of some form of absolute monarchy.

And from this point we start afresh, and begin the same business over again, with sundry fresh interludes.

All this is highly amusing to the English public to *hear* and *read* of; but I doubt whether our countrymen would like to be actual *performers* in such a drama.

Whether the French really are so, or whether they are mystifying us in the accounts they send over, I will not presume to decide. But if the former supposition be the true one,—if they have been so long really acting over and over again in their own persons such a drama, it must be allowed that they deserve to be characterized as they have been in the description given of certain European nations: "An Englishman," it has been said, "is never happy but when he is miserable; a Scotchman is never at home but when he is abroad; an Irishman is never at peace but when he is fighting; a Spaniard is never at liberty but when he is enslaved; and a Frenchman is never settled but when he is engaged in a revolution."

Besides the many strange and improbable circumstances in the history of Buonaparte that have been noticed in the foregoing pages, there are many others that have been omitted, two of which it may be worth while to advert to.

One of the most incredible is the received account of the persons known as the "Detenus." It is well known that a great number of English gentlemen passed many years, in the early part of the present century, abroad;—by their own account, in France. Their statement was, that while travelling in that country for their amusement as peaceable tourists, they were, on the sudden breaking out of a war, seized by this terrible Buonaparte, and kept prisoners for about twelve years, contrary to all the usages of civilized nations,—to all principles of justice, of humanity, of enlightened policy; many of them thus wasting in captivity the most important portion of their lives, and having all their prospects blighted.

Now whether these persons were in reality exiles by choice, for the sake of keeping out of the way of creditors, or of enjoying the society of those they preferred to their own domestic circle, I do not venture to conjecture. But let the reader consider whether *any* conjecture can be *more* improbable than the statement actually made.

It is, indeed, credible that ambition may prompt an unscrupulous man to make the most enormous sacrifices of human life, and to perpetrate the most atrocious crimes, for the advancement of his views of conquest. But that this *great* man—as he is usually reckoned even by adversaries—this hero according to some—this illustrious warrior, and mighty sovereign—should have stooped to be guilty of an act of mean and petty malice worthy of a spiteful old woman,—a piece of paltry cruelty which could not at all conduce to his success in the war, or produce any effect except to degrade his country, and exasperate ours;—this, surely, is quite incredible. "Pizarro," says Elvira in Kotzebue's play, "if not always justly, at least act always greatly."

But a still more wonderful circumstance connected with this transaction remains behind. A large portion of the English nation, and among these the whole of the Whig party, are said to have expressed the most vehement indignation, mingled with compassion, at the banishment from Europe, and confinement in St. Helena, of this great man. No considerations of regard for the peace and security of our own country, no dread of the power of so able and indefatigable a warrior, and so inveterate an enemy, should have induced us, they thought, to subject this formidable personage to a confinement, which was far less severe than that to which he was said to have subjected such numbers of our countrymen, the harmless *non-belligerent* travellers, whom (according to the story) he kidnapped in France, with no object but to gratify the basest and most unmanly spite.

But that there is no truth in that story, and that it was not believed by those who manifested so much sympathy and indignation on this great man's account, is sufficiently proved by that very sympathy and indignation.

There are again other striking improbabilities connected with the Polish nation in the history before us. Buonaparte is represented as having always expressed the strongest sympathy with that ill-used people; and they, as being devotedly attached to him, and fighting with the utmost fidelity and bravery in his armies, in which some of them attained high commands. Now he had it manifestly in his power at one period (according to the received accounts), with a stroke of his pen, to re-establish Poland as an independent state. For, in his last Russian war, he had complete occupation of the country (of which the population was perfectly friendly); the Russian portion of it was his by right of conquest; and Austria and Prussia, then his allies, and almost his subjects, would gladly have resigned their portions in exchange for some of the provinces they had ceded to France, and which were, to him, of little value, but, to them, important. And, indeed, Prussia was (as we are told) so thoroughly humbled and weakened, that he might easily have enforced the cession of Prussian-Poland, even without any compensation. And the re-establishment of the Polish kingdom would have been as evidently politic as it was reasonable. The independence of a faithful and devoted ally, at enmity with the surrounding nations—the very nations that were the most likely to combine (as they often had done) against him,—this would have given him, at no cost, a kind of strong garrison to maintain his power, and keep his enemies in check.

Yet this most obvious step, the history tells us, he did not take; but made flattering speeches to the Poles, used their services, and did nothing for them!

This is, alone, sufficiently improbable. But we are required moreover to believe that the Poles,—instead of *execrating* this man, who had done them the unpardonable wrong of wantonly disappointing the expectations he had, for his own purposes, excited, thus adding treachery to ingratitude—instead of this, continued to the last as much devoted to him as ever, and even now idolize his memory! We are to believe, in short, that this Buonaparte, not only in his own conduct and adventures violated all the established rules of probability, but also caused all other persons, as many as came in contact with him, to act as no mortals ever did act before: may we not add, as no mortals ever did act at all?

Many other improbabilities might be added to the list, and will be found in the complete edition of that history, from which some extracts have been given in the foregoing pages, and which has been published (under the title of "Historic Certainties") by Aristarchus Newlight, with a learned commentary (not, indeed, adopting the views contained in the foregoing pages, but) quite equal in ingenuity to a late work on the "Hebrew Monarchy."

THE END.

HISTORIC CERTAINTIES

RESPECTING THE

EARLY HISTORY OF AMERICA,

DEVELOPED IN A CRITICAL

EXAMINATION

OF THE BOOK OF THE CHRONICLES

OF THE LAND OF ECNARF.

BY

REV. ARISTARCHUS NEWLIGHT,

PHIL. DR. OF THE UNIVERSITY OF GIESSEN;
CORRESPONDING MEMBER
OF THE THEOPHILANTHROPIC AND PANTISOCRATICAL
SOCIETIES OF LEIPSIC;
LATE PROFESSOR OF ALL RELIGIONS IN
SEVERAL DISTINGUISHED ACADEMIES
AT HOME AND ABROAD,
ETC., ETC., ETC.

"Here, then, we have the rule: in cases where the details of an adventure are obnoxious to criticism, and where its exterior mechanism is exaggerated--where the basis itself is not conformable to reason, or where it is obviously made to agree with pre-existing ideas--in these cases, I say, not only the circumstances described with such precision, but the entire adventure, should be considered as *non-historic*. On the other hand, in those cases in which only the form of the narrative is impressed with the mythic character, whilst its basis is left untouched, it is possible to suppose an *historic nucleus*."—Strauss, *Leben Jesu*.

To

THE LEARNED AND ENLIGHTENED PUBLIC

OF EUROPE AND AMERICA,

SPECIALLY

TO THOSE EMINENT CRITICS,

AT HOME AND ABROAD,

WHOSE LABOURS UPON JEWISH HISTORY

I HAVE HUMBLY MADE

MY MODEL:

TO
DR. W.M. LEBERECHT DE WETTE,
DR. D.F. STRAUSS,
MR. F.W. NEWMAN,

THESE PAGES ARE INSCRIBED,

BY THEIR FAITHFUL SERVANT,

THE COMMENTATOR.

Sicily, April 1.

ADVERTISEMENT.

These "Chronicles" were first seen by me in November, 1850. The greater part of the MS. from which they are taken, was, however, in possession of the person from whom I received them so early as 1814; the remainder in the ensuing year. Should any number of competent judges feel doubts concerning the great antiquity of these Chronicles, and their American origin, I am sure that all such doubts will be removed by an inspection of the original, which may *then* be reasonably demanded.

HISTORIC CERTAINTIES.

THE BOOK OF THE CHRONICLES OF THE LAND OF ECNARF.

CHAP. I.

In the days of Egroeg king of Niatirb did king Sivol reign over Ecnarf, even as his fathers had reigned before him. The same was a just man and merciful. And the people, even the Ecnarfites, came and stood before Sivol, and said, Behold thy fathers made our yoke very grievous; now therefore make thou the heavy yoke of thy fathers which they put upon us, lighter; and give us statutes and ordinances that be righteous, like unto those of Niatirb; and we will serve thee; and the king did as they required. Then the Ecnarfites laid hands on king Sivol, and slew him and all his house, and all his great men, as many as they could find. But some fled in ships, and gat them away to Niatirb, and dwelt in Niatirb.

And the Ecnarfites said, Let us now have no king neither ruler over us, but let us do every one as seemeth right in his own eyes; then shall we be free, and we will set free the other nations also.

Then the king of Niatirb, and divers other kings, even the chief among all the rulers of Eporue, made war with one accord against the Ecnarfites, because they had slain the king; for they said, Lest our people also slay us.

In those days the Ecnarfites were in a great strait: for they had chosen councils of elders, and set judges over them; and some of the people followed one judge and some another; and they fought one against another many days. So the land was defiled with blood; for the Ecnarfites slew one another with a great slaughter. Moreover there was a sore dearth in the land, and the people were greatly impoverished. And the princes of Eporue also came and fought against Ecnarf. So the Ecnarfites went out and fought against them, and smote them, and prevailed against them exceedingly on every side. So they enlarged their boundaries greatly, over Ailati to the south, and until thou come to the river Sunehr towards the sunrising: and they smote the Namregs also that dwelt beyond Sunehr, and subdued Aivatab and Aiteoleh, and divers other countries of Eporue. So the Ecnarfites became a great people.

And it came to pass that they oppressed the nations round about them very grievously, and caused them to pay tribute of corn, and cattle, and silver and gold. So those nations made a league together, and rose up against the Ecnarfites many times: but they were utterly discomfited, until they were brought very low.

Nevertheless, the Ecnarfites prevailed not against the Niatirbites, because they dwelt in an island, and the king of Niatirb also had exceeding many ships of war. Howbeit, when they fought on land, the Ecnarfites prevailed, but when they fought by sea, the Niatirbites prevailed.

Now there was a certain man of Akisroc whose name was Noel-Opan: he was a mighty man of valour, and he was one of the chief captains of the host of the people of Ecnarf. And he gathered together a great host, and went and fought against Sutpyge, and overcame the princes of the land, whom the ruler of Yekrut had set over it. And when the king of Niatirb heard thereof, he sent ships of war and valiant men to fight against the Ecnarfites in Sutpyge. And Noel-Opan drew nigh unto the city of Erca and fought against it. But there were certain of the Niatirbites therein, which strengthened the hands of the people of the city, and drove back Noel-Opan, and slew many of his people: so he fled from before that place.

And after that, the great host of the Niatirbites came to Sutpyge, and warred against the Ecnarfites that were there; and over-threw them, and smote them with a great slaughter, and took them captive, until they had left them none remaining. Thus were the Ecnarfites destroyed out of Sutpyge. Howbeit Noel-Opan had left the captains and the army that were in Sutpyge, and fled, and returned back to Ecnarf. Then the Ecnarfites took Noel-Opan, and made him ruler over them. So Noel-Opan became exceeding great, inasmuch that there was none like him, of all that had ruled over Ecnarf before him.

CHAP. II.

Now it came to pass that when Noel-Opan was made ruler of Ecnarf, he sent a letter unto the king of

Niatirb, saying, Let us now make peace. But the king said, Thou art a rebel and a murderer; I will have no peace with thee. Howbeit after a time they made peace together.

But when the king of Niatirb saw that Noel-Opan waxed exceeding strong, he stirred up the other princes of Eporue, and they fought against Ecnarf both by sea and land. Then was Noel-Opan wroth, and he gathered together a very great host, and built ships, and said, Surely I will bring an army against thee across the sea, and will smite thee and thy people with the edge of the sword, and take their goods for a prey. Nevertheless he came not; for the ships of Niatirb kept watch round all the coasts of Ecnarf, that none might come in or go out. And the Niatirbite ships prevailed against the Ecnarfite ships, and overthrew them utterly. But Noel-Opan smote all the country of his enemies that was on that side of the sea, and smote them with the edge of the sword; his eye did not pity them. And he took their fenced cities, and made his chief captains, and those of his own house, rulers in the countries which he subdued; and he made their yoke very grievous.

Now there was peace between Noel-Opan, ruler of Ecnarf, and Zednanref, king of Niaps. And Noel-Opan said unto Zednanref, Come into my country to me, and I will show thee kindness. So when he came, Noel-Opan took him and put him in ward, and kept him in bonds many days; and sent his own brother Phesoi to be king over Niaps.

Then the Niapsites cried unto the king of Niatirb, and he sent an army, and fought against Phesoi, even until he had thrust him out from being king. And

Noel-Opan sent back Zednanref, and he returned and ruled over Niaps.

Now there were certain of the Niapsites which had taken part with Phesoi and with the Ecnarfites, and had fought against Zednanref. And when Zednanref was restored unto his kingdom, he took these men and promoted them to be judges and captains and councillors in the kingdom of Niaps: but the men that had fought for him, and brought him back unto his own land, these did he afflict very grievously, and slew divers of them, and others he thrust into prison, and spoiled them of their goods, and made bondsmen of them. Thus did Zednanref unto his people.

Now the Niatirbites were a very wealthy people, and had much merchandise; for they were cunning workmen in wool, and in iron, and in brass; and they had many ships also, which brought home of the good things of the East and of the West, even very precious merchandise. And the Ecnarfites and the rest of the servants of Noel-Opan traded with them, because it was for their profit; so they bought raiment, and works of iron and of brass, and spices, and goodly fruits of the East and of the West, of the merchants of Niatirb. Then Noel-Opan commanded his officers, and they sought out all the goods which the servants of Noel-Opan had bought, and burned them with fire, and destroyed them utterly. Thus did Noel-Opan continually. Moreover he sent also unto the rulers of Ai-Namreg and the other rulers of Eporue, and said unto them, As ye have seen me do, even so do ye; and they obeyed his voice, and sent and destroyed all the goods which were brought into their land, even very much merchandise. Only Rednaxela ruler of Aissur would not hearken unto Noel-Opan.

Then Noel-Opan ruler of Ecnarf, and Sicnarf ruler of Saturia, and Egul-Sumli ruler of Assurpi, and all the princes of Ai-Namreg, gathered themselves together, they and all their people, and went and fought against Aissur. Now the Aissurites were mighty men of valour; nevertheless they could not stand against Noel-Opan, because he had a very great host, even as the sands that are upon the seashore for multitude; he had exceeding many horses also, and instruments of war; and his captains were mighty men of valour. So he went forward and smote the western parts of the land of Aissur with the edge of the sword, and burned their houses with fire, and defiled their temples; and he laid waste all the country of Aissur until he came even unto Vocsom, which is the chief of all their cities. Then the Aissurites set fire to Vocsom and burned it. Then Noel-Opan sent messengers unto Rednaxela, saying, Let us now make peace together. But all the great men of Aissur said unto Rednaxela, Hearken not unto Noel-Opan, neither make thou any covenant with him, so long as one man of all his host remaineth in our land. Is he not come up to make all thy people servants unto the Ecnarfites? Else, if thou do in any wise hearken unto his words, we will surely slay thee, even as we slew the Ruler that was before thee. So Rednaxela answered nothing unto the messengers, but sent forth his men of war to fight against Noel-Opan. Then Noel-Opan departed, he and all his people; for they said, Lest the host perish with the cold and with the famine.

Then Rednaxela ruler of Aissur, he and all his people, went and pursued the Ecnarfites, and the Saturians, and the Aissurpites, and the rest of the host that was with Noel-Opan, and smote them with an exceeding great slaughter; and chased them out of the land. So the host was utterly discomfited; for they were more that died by the snow and by the famine than those which the men of Aissur slew with the edge of the sword. And Noel-Opan fled for his life. Then Votalp, who was one of the captains of the host of Rednaxela, made proclamation, saying, Whosoever shall slay Noel-Opan, or shall take him alive, he shall receive an hundred thousand pieces of silver, and I will give him my daughter to wife. Nevertheless Noel-Opan escaped, and returned and dwelt at Sirap.

CHAP. III.

And it came to pass after these things that Noel-Opan strengthened himself, and gathered together another host, instead of that which he had lost, and went and warred against the Aissurpites, and the Aissurites, and the Saturians, and all the rulers of the north country which were confederate against him. And the ruler of Nedews also, which was an Ecnarfite, warred against Noel-Opan. So they went forth and fought against the Ecnarfites in the plain of Gispiel. And the Ecnarfites were discomfited before their enemies, and fled, and came to the rivers which are behind Gispiel, and essayed to pass over, that they might escape out of the hand of their enemies; but they could not; for Noel-Opan had destroyed the bridges. So the people of the north country came upon them, and smote them with a very grievous slaughter.

But Noel-Opan and those that were with him came unto the bridge that was left (for he spared one of the bridges and destroyed it not), and they passed over, and escaped, and fled towards their own land. And their enemies pursued after them. Then the king of Ai-Ravab, whom Noel-Opan had made king of Ai-Ravab, came out to stop the way against the Ecnarfites, to the intent they might not escape into their own land. So there was a very sore battle that day; and much people of the Ecnarfites were slain; howbeit, Noel-Opan and they that were with him broke through the host of the Ai-Ravabites, and came unto their own land.

Then the ruler of Saturia and all the rulers of the north country sent messengers to Noel-Opan to speak peaceably unto him, saying, Why should there be war between us any more? Now Noel-Opan had put away his wife, and taken the daughter of the ruler of Saturia to wife. So all the councillors of Noel-Opan, even all his wise men, came and said unto Noel-Opan, Behold now, these kings are merciful kings: do even as they say unto thee; knowest thou not yet that Ecnarf is destroyed? But he spake roughly unto his councillors, and drove them out from his presence, neither would he hearken unto their voice. And when all the kings saw that, they warred against Ecnarf, and smote it with the edge of the sword: as the Ecnarfites had done to Aissur, even so did the

Aissurites to Ecnarf: only their cities did they not burn, neither did they defile their temples.

And they came near unto Sirap, which is the royal city, to take it. And they fought against it, and prevailed against the men of war which had set themselves in array before the city, and drove them back into the city. Then all the men of Sirap said one to another, Behold, all these nations are come against us, to afflict us, even as we have afflicted them; and we have no strength to stand against them: let us now go out and make supplication unto them: peradventure they will save our lives. So they went out and delivered up the city unto them. Then those kings spake kindly unto the men of Sirap, saying, Be of good cheer, there shall no harm happen unto you.

Then the men of Sirap were glad, and said, What have we to do with Noel-Opan? He shall not rule over us any longer. Also all the princes, the judges, the councillors, and the captains, whom Noel-Opan had raised up, even of the lowest of the people, sent unto Sivol the brother of Sivol king of Ecnarf, whom they had slain, saying, Noel-Opan is a tyrant and a murderer, and we have thrust him out from being our ruler: only the honours and the rewards and the offices which he hath given us, those will we keep; if therefore thou wilt let us keep all these things, thou shalt be our king. And Sivol was glad, and he arose and went to Ecnarf to be king over them. Now there were divers great men in Ecnarf, men of renown, who had behaved themselves valiantly and fought against Sivol, and his house, and against the kings which took part with him: all these did Noel-Opan greatly reward, and promoted them to be chiefs over the people. So all these men took Sivol and made him king over Ecnarf; and they were made princes, and councillors, and judges, and chief captains under him.

And when Noel-Opan saw that the kingdom was departed from him, he said unto the ruler of Saturia, and the other rulers which came against him, Let me, I pray you, give the kingdom unto my son: but they would not hearken unto him. Then he spake yet again, saying, Let me, I pray you, go and live in Abel; and ye shall give me an allowance for me and my household, and the land of Abel also for a possession. So they sent him to Abel, and Noel-Opan dwelt at Abel, and ruled over it. To his brethren also, and to his mother, they gave silver and gold. But the wife of Noel-Opan, even the daughter of the ruler of Saturia, whom he had married, she and the son that she bore to Noel-Opan, received an inheritance of the hand of her father in the land of Ai-Lati: So she saw the face of her husband no more.

CHAP. IV.

In those days there arose a sore famine in the land of Yavron, which is in the North Sea, over against Kramned. And it came to pass on this wise: the king of Kramned, who is the king of Yavron, was at peace with the other rulers of Eporue; and Noel-Opan, ruler of Ecnarf, said unto Rednaxela, ruler of Aissur, Behold the king of Kramned hath ships; go to, let us cause his ships to fight for us against the king of

Niatirb; peradventure we may prevail over him. And Rednaxela, ruler of Aissur, hearkened unto the words of Noel-Opan; so they conspired together. But when the king of Niatirb heard thereof, he sent and took away the ships of the king of Kramned. Then was the king of Kramned wroth, and warred against the king of Niatirb. And the ruler of Aissur, even Rednaxela, and the ruler of Nedews also, which was an Ecnarfite, helped the Niatirbites against the Kramnedites and Ecnarfites: so the king of Niatirb kept the ships which the ruler of Ecnarf and the ruler of Aissur had thought to bring against him.

And the ruler of Nedews said unto the king of Kramned, Give me now Yavron, because it is nigh unto my country; and I will make a league with thee, that we may fight against the Ecnarfites. So when the king of Kramned saw that he was in evil plight, he said, Be content, take Yavron; so he made a league with him. But the men of Yavron said, We will not serve the ruler of Nedews. So they set a king over them, and strengthened themselves against the Nedewsites. And they said unto the ruler of Niatirb, Behold thy people is a free people; and ye have also delivered the Niapsites out of the hands of their oppressors; let us, we pray thee, be free also; and suffer thy people to bring us corn in ships, for money, that we may eat bread; for we have not food enough. But the ruler of Niatirb said, Nay, but ye shall serve the ruler of Nedews. So he gave commandment to all the captains of his ships that they should suffer no corn to be carried into the land of Yavron. Thus it came to pass that the famine was grievous in the land of Yavron. And the ruler of Nedews prevailed against the Yavronites, and bare rule over them.

And it came to pass at this time, that Apap returned unto his own land. Now the Ecnarfites, and divers other nations of Eporue, are servants of Apap, and hold him in reverence; but he is an abomination to the Niatirbites, and to the Aissurites, and to the Aissurpites, and to the Nedewsites. Howbeit the Ecnarfites had taken away all his lands, and stripped him of all that he had, and carried him away captive into Ecnarf. But when the Niatirbites, and the Aissurites, and the Aissurpites, and the Nedewsites, and the rest of the nations that were confederate against Ecnarf, came thither, they caused the Ecnarfites to set Apap at liberty, and to restore all his goods that they had taken: likewise they gave him back all his lands; and he went home in peace, and ruled over his own city, as in times past.

CHAP. V.

And it came to pass after these things, when Noel-Opan had not yet been a full year in Abel, that he said unto his men of war which clave unto him, Go to, let us go back to Ecnarf, and fight against king Sivol, and thrust him out from being king. So he departed, he and six hundred men with him that drew the sword, and warred against king Sivol. Then all the men of Belial gathered themselves together and said, God save Noel-Opan. And when Sivol heard that, he fled and gat him into Muigleb; and Noel-Opan ruled over Ecnarf.

And he sent unto the ruler of Niatirb, and unto all the rulers of Eporue, saying, Let me, I pray you, rule over Ecnarf, and let there be peace between me and you. But they would not hearken unto him; but gathered together an exceeding great host to fight against him. Then Noel-Opan, he and all his mighty men of valour, went out and fought against the Niatirbites and the Aissurpites and the Muiglebites, in the plain country of Muigleb. And there was a very sore battle that day; and the Niatirbites prevailed against the Ecnarfites, and smote them with a very grievous slaughter. Then Noel-Opan fled, and returned to Sirap; but the people thrust him out from being ruler over them. So he went and gave himself up into the hands of the Niatirbites, and said, I pray you let me dwell in your country. But they sent him away to another island, in a far country, and set a watch over him, even armed men, and ships of war on every side. And king Sivol returned to Ecnarf and ruled over the Ecnarfites, as his fathers had reigned in time past.

COMMENTARY.

CHAP. I.

This curious document has lately come into my possession, in a way which I am not at present quite at liberty to explain. A small fragment of it has already been printed by the ingenious author of *Historic Doubts respecting Napoleon Buonaparte*, who, taking advantage of a striking parallel between this story and some supposed recent events, altered the ancient names[*] for modern ones. The parallel is no doubt

---

[*]With respect to these names, which might at first sight seem a little suspicious, I must request the reader to suspend his judgement. A distinguished Irish antiquary, whose labours are known and valued as they deserve through all Europe, has assured me that he finds traces of them in the Eugubian tables, and cognate inscriptions in the Ogham character. The name of Niatirb is probably compounded of נא, or, in the *plenior scriptio*, ניא or גוא (י and ו being originally the same letter), which occurs in such names of places as No-ammon (Nahum iii. 8), &c. &c., which probably denotes dwelling, abode (compare ναίειν, ναὸς), and מרף, the name of the god of spoil (cf. Ps. lxxvi 5), or תרב (cf. Heb. תרבית), the god of *usury*—*i.e.* Plutus. Many things, indeed, make it probable that Gain was the deity chiefly worshipped in Niatirb. Similar traces of Hebrew radicals occur in the Book of Mormon, which has quite as large a substratum of fact as the Jewish histories. See in the *Studien und Kritiken* for 1843 (*Viertes Heft*, Hamburg, 1843), some curious evidence produced from Daumer (on the Moloch-worship of the ancient Hebrews) of an early connexion (through

curious; but, perhaps, more curious than just. But if
the hypothesis of that critic be correct, it may serve to
show that the framers of the legend of Buonaparte
worked upon a model already in existence, a phenomenon not unfrequent in myths. With this, however, I have no direct concern. The critic of whom I
speak, applying the philosophical principles of evidence, as a test, justly pronounced the story here
given *as a whole* incredible. It did not suit his purpose to go farther into details, nor, indeed, would the
coarse way of dealing with ancient narratives then in
fashion have favoured his doing so. But a more deli-
cate method of investigation has of late years been

Abraham) between Palestine and America. He has tried to
show (p. 260—in the Review, p. 1037), that the original name
of that continent was Noah. But it may be questioned whether
he has not mistaken the important isle Nia or Noa-Tirb for the
continent itself. The ludicrous attempt to identify the name
with *Britain* (by reading it backward!) can hardly be seriously
meant, and is worthy only of Dean Swift. Nor can that wild
attempt be even *consistently* carried out. What, e.g. can be
made of Saituria, and Egul-Sumli?   Yet these names may be
readily illustrated by the lights of the Indo-Semitic dialects.
Delitzsch (Jesurun, p. 220) has shown that *ûr*, in Sanskrit, *ura*,
is a proper Semitic termination, as in כפתדר from כפת and
צפור from צף. This gives זיתור, or, in the Sanskrit form, *Zai-
tura=Saituria*, as the "olive-land": and this shows us why the
Σάτυροι   were, in the Greek mythology, represented as the
companions of Bacchus; "wine and oil" being associated in the
ideas of the ancients.

Egul-Sumli is equivalent to the Latin name *Rorarius*, being
obviously derived from אגל, *dew* (Job xxxviii, 28), and סמל, *to
resemble*. Compare the Hebrew description of a good prince,—
   Like rain shall he fall upon the mown grass:
   Like the drops that bedew the soil.—*Psalm* lxxii 4.

introduced in Germany, which has enabled us to pre-
cipitate, as it were, a certain portion of truth from the
most romantic narratives, and make even mythic legends supply solid contributions to legitimate history. Such a method it is my wish to apply in the present instance, referring the reader for a minute de-
lineation of it to Strauss's admirable preface to the
Leben Jesu, and Mr. Newman's *History of the Hebrew Commonwealth*.

This document (though professing to be the
chronicles of Ecnarf) is plainly the work of a Niatirbite. It dates from the days of Egroeg, king of
Niatirb; and the design of exalting that island
(whether justly or not) is so manifest all through the
narrative, that it must strike the reader even at first
glance.

Taking, then, this clue with us, and reviewing the
whole document in the light of "the higher criticism,"
we shall find little difficulty in arriving at the substantial truth. Guided by a fixed ruling principle, we
shall discover that a consistent thread of fact lies at
the bottom of this tangled tissue, which may, in most
instances, be brought out entire, when sought for with
a keen eye and a steady hand.

The very opening of the narrative is full of contradictions, which at once betray their origin.

"Sivol," it is said, "was a just man and merciful."
We are told this in immediate connexion with the
statement that he ruled over Ecnarf, *"even as his* fathers had reigned before him." Yet, in the very next
sentence we find the people complaining that his fathers (these princes who had reigned like the just and
merciful Sivol) made their yoke very grievous; and

not only so, but plainly intimating that the yoke upon them still continued grievous under this just and merciful sovereign! But the purpose which was meant to be served by these flagrant contradictions soon reveals itself. The constitution of Niatirb is to be represented, at all hazards, as the envy and admiration of other people; and with that aim, the subjects are to be represented as importunately demanding its introduction. The issue however of king Sivol's supposed compliance with their demand sufficiently refutes both these absurd encomiums upon that constitution itself, and the account here given of its attempted introduction into Ecnarf. The people, we are informed, immediately upon receiving *the boon they sought*, "laid hands on king Sivol, and slew him, and all his house, and all his great men, and as many as they could find." Here we are called upon to believe that *precisely the same consequences as we might expect to attend the forcing of disagreeable laws on an unwilling people, attended the frank concession of a gift which that people earnestly desired.* This is surely too large a demand upon our credulity; and if, rejecting such a story as a palpable misrepresentation, we turn to consider what is likely to have been the real state of facts thus coloured by an interested narrator, the next clause will afford us material assistance. "But some fled in ships, and *got them away to* Niatirb, and *dwelt* in Niatirb." We see here it was *the king's friends* who found their natural asylum in that island, whose laws, when introduced into Ecnarf, produced a revolution that overturned a very ancient dynasty, and occasioned the execution of the prince and his chief adherents. It needs no peculiar sagacity

to discern the truth through this almost transparent
veil of fiction. Sivol was just and merciful, because
he was the friend of Niatirb. *All*, we must observe,
who adhere to that island are *just** in the language of
this document; while *all* who oppose its interests are,
as a matter of course, depicted as monsters of cruelty
and perfidiousness. He attempted (perhaps he may
have coloured the attempt by bribing some of the
populace to demand it)—He attempted to force the
odious "laws and ordinances" of Niatirb upon a re-
luctant nation. His outraged subjects rose in defence
of their rights. Possibly he and his chief adherents
may have perished in the conflict. But that there was
no such wholesale massacre as the words at first
might seem to imply, the document itself makes evident, by confessing that *"some* fled in *ships"*
[observe the plural number], "and got them away to
Niatirb," where they naturally looked for, and naturally found, protection.

To any one who is thoroughly aware of the prejudiced tone of the narrative, the next paragraph will
sound as little more than the writer's peculiar way of
saying, that the Ecnarfites established a constitution
which, in its liberality, contrasted strongly with the
tyrannous government of the king of Niatirb and his
brother despots. The document itself makes it sufficiently plain that its statements cannot be taken as
literally true. For after telling us that the Ecnarfites

----

*So afterwards, "Behold these kings are *merciful* kings."
Michaelis (ad Lowth, *Prælcct.* p. 534) has remarked a similar
usage of the words "wicked" and "righteous" in the Hebrew
Scriptures.

had resolved to "do every one as seemed right in his own eyes," it incidentally admits that "they had chosen councils of elders and set judges over them." These are not the proceedings of a lawless mob; but it is no new thing for the bigoted admirers of monarchy to traduce all republican institutions as mere anarchy and confusion. And that this really lies at the bottom of the gross exaggeration before us, becomes more and more manifest as we proceed. The Ecnarfites, it is said, proposed not only to be free themselves, but to "set free other nations." Now, this supposes that, in their opinion, other nations were not *free*. And, throughout the whole of the document, it is not so much as once pretended that the nations on the *continent* of Eporue were free. On the contrary, it seems everywhere implied that the princes of the various people there enumerated were despots in the most odious sense of the term, and their subjects really slaves. The happy isle of Niatirb is the one exception; the laws of which are earnestly desired by suffering subjects as a light and easy yoke. Yet, no sooner do the Ecnarfites assert their freedom, than the king of Niatirb is seized with the same panic as the other princes. He makes common cause with them, and for the same reason. An *intention* of the enfranchised Ecnarfites to set other people free is, indeed, alleged; but no overt act of hostility on their part is specified. The contagious influence of their example, not the aggressive power of their armies, is manifestly the thing dreaded; "For they said, lest *our people* slay us." Truly, "it is conscience that makes cowards of us all." If the king of Niatirb had felt that his case was an excepted one, and that his people felt themselves under the administration of equal laws and in the enjoyment of political rights—that they were already what could with any propriety of speech be called a *free* people—he would never have given way to such unreasonable apprehensions; still less, if the visible effects of the revolution in Ecnarf were such as are here described:—"The Ecnarfites slew one another with a great slaughter. Moreover, there was a sore dearth in the land, and the people were greatly impoverished." What was there, let me ask, in the spectacle of such a state to seduce a *free* people, possessing already a liberal and just constitution—a people affluent, as we are told, chap. ii, in all the luxuries of life—to follow an example so disastrous in its consequences, and to follow which they had so few temptations?

Honesty, however, compels me to confess that I do not lay much stress upon the representation here given of the state of Ecnarf, as furnishing a ground for this argument, which is quite strong enough without it. That representation is chiefly worth attending to, as manifesting the *animus* of the narrator himself, who seems (under the usual prejudices of persons reared under despotism) to confound, or wish his readers to confound, the ideas of freedom and anarchy, and to recognize no distinction between oppression and licentiousness. No rational person, indeed, who ventures to examine for himself, can fail to perceive that the picture here drawn of the disturbances which may possibly have attended the sudden attainment of liberty in Ecnarf is, to say the least of it, grossly overcharged in the colouring. If that nation were indeed reduced by civil dissension and famine to

the condition here described, they *could not be* such
an object of terror to the surrounding people; nor
would their subjugation require the combined forces
of so many princes conspiring in a league against
them. But when it is added that a people thus weakened by mutual slaughter and famine not only resist
such potent assailants, but subdue them;—not only
protect their own soil, but carry their conquests far
and wide over the land of their enemies;—the story
sinks under its own inconsistencies. Still this does not
imply that we are to reject the whole as a pure fiction.
Let us cast away that which the writer had a manifest
object in mis-stating. His enmity to Ecnarf would not
lead him to magnify its successes, but it might well
lead him to falsify the history of its state under the
new *anti-Niatirbite* constitution. Discounting then, as
it were, this envious fiction, we shall find that the
facts elicited from his whole statement are as fol-
lows:—An endeavour to introduce the Laws of
Niatirb into Ecnarf was made in the reign of Sivol;
the consequence of that attempt was a general rising
of the people, in which Sivol and his principal adherents lost their lives, the remainder flying into Niatirb,
where they were received as friends. Thereupon the
Ecnarfites resolved to be free, and established a government by Councils of Elders and Judges. In consequence of these proceedings the king of Niatirb, and
other princes of Eporue, became alarmed lest their
subjects should follow the example of the Ecnarfites,
and formed a league for the purpose of crushing
them. Nevertheless, the state of Ecnarf became so
strong, under its new institutions, that is not only re-

sisted their assault, but extended its dominion over a large portion of the continent of Eporue.

These, I say, are *the simple facts* presented by the document itself. I have not *added a single tittle* to the statements made by the chronicler. I have only removed some manifestly inconsistent and exaggerated representations introduced for an obvious purpose, by which they were overlaid. And I think I may safely leave it to the intelligent reader himself to draw the proper inference from these *facts*. We have now then gained at last firm footing, and may proceed, with less hesitating steps, to make our way through the quaking mire of falsehood and misrepresentation which surrounds us.

The next paragraph—making allowance as before for hostile *colouring*—may be allowed to have a basis of fact. The Ecnarfites probably found it necessary to levy such contributions as are usually levied by conquerors in the countries occupied by their troops; which may also have been greatly inconvenient to a people already impoverished by the oppressive exactions of their native princes.

There is much internal probability also in the next statement. Islands have ever been famous (since the days of Minos) for their naval power; and the Niatirbites may, very likely, have had such an advantage by sea over their continental neighbours as is here described. The frank admission that their forces were inferior by land, adds to the verisimilitude of the narrative. But I shall show presently that, as we might expect, their success in naval warfare was not so absolutely *uniform* as this writer would have us to believe. Taken, however, with the requisite abatements, this paragraph also may be admitted as a statement of facts.

But the complexion of the next statement will justify greater hesitation.

A person (Noel-Opan)* now enters upon the scene, whom it is the manifest wish of this writer to hold up as an object of dread and aversion to the people of Niatirb.

The rules of evidence, therefore, demand that we should watch his proceedings jealously when dealing with such a character; and remembering that we have no contemporary Ecnarfite counter-statement to set against his prejudiced testimony, give that nation the benefit of any doubt which may be raised by the tenour of the narrative. We should deal, in short, as if we were handling a Hebrew priest's uncorroborated account of the Baal-worshippers, or a Davidite's description of the kingdom of Israel. Bearing, then, all this in mind, let us examine the statement before us.

---

*This, I have no doubt, was not his real name, but the *nick-name* under which he was known in Niatirb. Noel-Opan is neither more nor less than the "Godless Revolution." נוּב as Gesenius justly observes, is radically equivalent to *verneinen, vernichten*, to deny or annihilate. As a particle, it answers to the Greek negative, νη (in νῆπιος, νημερτῆς, &c.)—the Latin *ne* or *non*—the English *no*—the German *nein*—the Arabic ﻝ. EL (אֵל) as every one knows, is the name of God: Noel therefore is the same as αθεος, godless. אוֹפָן, Opan, actually occurs as the name of a *wheel* in Ezekiel, in Exod. xiv 25, and many other places. In its contracted form, אֹפַן, it denotes a *period or revolution* of time. It is impossible to resist these little obvious, but on that account more striking, evidences of the antiquity of the document. The framers of the story of Napoleon were, I fancy, aware of the true etymology of Noel-Opan. Hence they represent a great literary bugbear (Lord Byron) as signing his name, Noel-Byron,"—just as *Shelley* is said to have written αθεος after his name in the album at Chamouni.

"There was a certain man of Akisroc, whose name was Noel-Opan." In another MS I find the remarkable addition, "a man *of the island* of Akisroc." This great man, then, was an *islander*, and therefore, as we have seen, not unlikely to supply the Ecnarfites with what they most needed,—an officer well skilled in the management of fleets. If we admit this easy hypothesis, it will account for much that might otherwise seem startling in the narrative. It will show us how one, not a native Ecnarfite, should attain such eminence as is here attributed to the Akisrocan Noel-Opan, or personification of the Godless Revolution. He and his islanders now take the lead, because the State is engaged in naval affairs, in which the Ecnarfites were notoriously deficient; for that the war in Sutpyge *involved*, at least, large marine operations, is evident (though that fact is industriously obscured) from the language of the narrative, where it tells us, that the king of Niatirb "sent *ships of war* and valiant men to fight against the Ecnarfites." Again: this hypothesis will account for the Ecnarfites now venturing on a distant naval expedition, a step which would be otherwise highly improbable, considering their previous frequent reverses at sea.

I think we may fairly assume, then, that this expedition to Sutpyge was principally a naval expedition, if not wholly such. Certainly, whatever is here told us of land operations is little more than pure fable. It is quite impossible to believe that the presence of "*certain* of the Niatirbites" in Erca, should have been sufficient to defeat such a chieftain as Noel-Opan, when we know, from this writer's own admission, that the Niatirbites were, even in large armies, quite inferior by land to Ecnarfite soldiers. But if there were really no considerable land-operations in this war, of which any true records remained, here was precisely just one of those blank spaces which the mythic fancy loves to fill with imaginary incidents. Where there were *real* battles by land, even this historian cannot pretend that the Niatirbites reaped many laurels; but, to save their credit, he conjures up in a distant region a fantastic campaign of his own, where they may safely enjoy—

Occulta spolia et plures de pace triumphos.

Nor does it militate against this view, that we find that Noel-Opan overcame the Princes *of the land* of Sutpyge. Those princes (if there were any such) were the deputies of a foreign Sovereign, the ruler of Yekrut. It is natural to suppose that the native population were ready enough to rise against them; so that nothing more was necessary than the reduction of their fortresses, (situated most likely on the seacoast,) and the supply of arms to the natives of the country. All this might be effected by a naval expedition.

The expedition then, I repeat, was almost entirely a *naval* one; and it seems equally certain that it was *successful*. The historian, indeed, assures us, that "Noel-Opan left the captains and the army, and fled." But what I have before said will readily account for the former statement, and what he himself adds sufficiently refutes the latter.

That Noel-Opan returned *without* an army is, I think, a fact. The prejudiced chronicler *accounts* for this fact in his own peculiar way, by saying that he *left the army behind*. But if I am right, the reader sees that we do not need any forced *account* of the matter at all. He returned without an army, because he had gone without an army.

Now, secondly, as to his flight. He must have fled, if he fled at all, *by sea*. Indeed, my MS. says expressly—"and fled away *in ships*." But we do not need that help. This point has been proved already, Now, we may ask, how could he possibly have *escaped* in this way? The King of Niatirb, we are told, was undisputed master of the sea. He had "exceeding many ships of war," nay, his fleet is described in Chap. II, as watching "round *all the coasts* of Ecnarf, that *none* might come in or go out." Plainly Noel-Opan could only have *escaped* such a guard as this by *conquering* it.[*]

---

[*]To these arguments we may add another philological one, which (as less certain in itself) I reserve for a note. In the name Sutpyge, the first syllable is evidently equivalent to our *South*, Germ. *Süd*—, which appears transposed in the Latin Aust-er— *Saut-er:* while the other syllable is as plainly connected with the Semitic צוס, *frigere*. The name, then, indicates some region near or within the Antarctic Circle; which could hardly be valuable but as a naval or fishing station. Yekrut connects itself with ירק, (in the form ירקות cf. ברות, from ברה) "to be green." I understand by it, some of the verdant Australian regions: but the great antiquary before referred to thinks that it plainly indicates "the *Emerald* Isle"—"the *green* Isle of the West." It must be allowed that the story of St. Brandan's voyages, and the legend of O'Brazil, seem to show a very early connection between Ireland and the New World. But *penes lectorem esto judicium*. The great *distance* of Yekrut, on this hypothesis, would sufficiently account for our hearing no more of its monarch in the rest of the history, and for his leaving the defence of

And that conquer it he did, is still more demonstratively evident from the result. "Then the Ecnarfites took Noel-Opan, and made him ruler over them." This is *not* the return which people make to a baffled chieftain, and that chieftain a stranger, who has basely abandoned his captains and his army, and brings back nothing but the fatal consequences of disaster, and the indelible shame of defeat; but it *is* the recompence which a grateful people might well bestow upon a victorious warrior, who has restored power where there had been weakness—who has humbled the boasting enemy in his own element, and by some hardly-hoped-for success, achieved imperishable renown for himself and for his adopted country.

CHAP. II.

With what precise powers Noel-Opan was invested, on becoming "Ruler of Ecnarf," it would be difficult, perhaps impossible, to discover. We shall find, however, substantial proofs hereafter, that his authority was not *despotical*, but limited by a constitution acceptable to the country. His office was very probably somewhat similar to that of a modern "President," or "Doge," and an ancient "Archon," or "Consul." Immediately upon his elevation, we find him (in a manner wholly inconsistent with the ambitious and overbearing character here attributed to him) making vol-

---

Sutpyge wholly to his ally, the king of Niatirb.

untary overtures of peace to the king of Niatirb, and
persisting in them too, in spite of the contemptuous
manner in which they were at first received. He felt,
no doubt, the strength and lustre of his own position;
and in the glory of his late victories, and with the
united support of a grateful nation, he could afford to
despise the petty insolence of an irritated, because
humbled, antagonist. He was resolved to restore tranquillity to the Continent; and he was conscious of
having the power to coerce the Niatirbites, if necessary, to come to reasonable terms. The king of
Niatirb, after some blustering, soon showed that he
also understood the nature of the crisis; and, after a
period of negotiation, peace at last was made.

Peace, however, which was sincerely desired by
Noel-Opan for his own sake, was regarded by the
king of Niatirb merely as a breathing-space to pre-
pare for a fresh and more desperate struggle;

"Mox reficit rates
Quassas."

We find him soon once more in the possession of a
numerous and powerful navy. But (in a manner quite
at variance with the story of his recent wonderful
victories over the Ecnarfite army in Sutpyge) he
trusts wholly for *land-forces* to the assistance of his
continental allies, whom he perfidiously "stirs up"
against Noel-Opan, during the very peace which that
ruler's clemency had granted. No wonder that, under
such circumstances, Noel-Opan should be "wroth,"
and resolve to crush for ever so troublesome and
faithless an enemy. That the delay of his expedition

into Niatirb was wholly owing (as this chronicler would fain persuade us) to the watchfulness of its fleets, is hardly credible. It seems much more probable that the great Ecnarfite commander was diverted from that object by the more pressing assaults of his immediate assailants on shore. I need not warn the reader to set down as exaggerations the account given of Noel-Opan's hard treatment of his enemies. We are by this time prepared for such statements, and refer them, as a matter of course, to their real origin.

How far the chronicler was prepared to go in the way of misrepresentation, we have a striking instance, in the story of Zednanref. At first sight, it appears one monstrous mass of glaring falsehoods and contradictions; but, on a nearer view, the way clears, and a remarkable paragraph at the end puts the clue into our hand, which we may safely follow.

Zednanref, we are there told, upon his return to Niaps* rewarded the adherents of Phesoi, and punished those persons who, during his absence, had

-----

*Niaps is clearly a Hebrew or Phoenician formative. גרא, as we have already seen, is a *local* prefix. אפס denotes an *extremity*; and it occurs as part of the name of a place in the tribe of Judah, 1 Sam. xvii. 1. Niaps was probably an extreme peninsula of Eporue. If we take גי אפ אש as the true expression, and suppose אפ אש (lit. *the nose of fire*) to denote a volcano, we may identify Niaps with the *Terra del Fuego* of modern geographers. To this latter hypothesis I rather incline. Eporue (compare the modern *Peru* and ancient *Ophir*, and the dual form, פרוים, *Parvayim*—i.e. *the two Perus*, or North and South America, 2 Chron. iii. 6) will then be fixed as *South America*. The Yncas or Ycnas were possibly an Ecnarfite dynasty, the heavy final syllable of Ecnarf dropping its consonants, to lighten the pronunciation.

taken up arms in his name. As it is confessed that he
was, at this time at least, perfectly a free agent, we
cannot construe such a proceeding otherwise than as
a deliberate declaration on his part, that he regarded
Phesoi's friends as *his* friends, and Phesoi's enemies
as *his* enemies. The story, then, of his having been
entrapped by Noel-Opan, and kept a prisoner in Ecnarf, vanishes of itself. But we may go farther. The
crafty king of Niatirb would never have sent out a
large army into Niaps for the mere unselfish purpose
of restoring the legitimate monarch to his rights. He
must have designed (if any such expedition were
made at all) to establish his own, and destroy the influence of Noel-Opan in that quarter. Is it credible,
then, that he should have permitted this mere puppet-
prince, restored by the force of the Niatirbite arms, to
follow (even if he were absurdly so inclined) a policy
fatal to the very objects for which he had expended so
much blood and treasure?

> "Credat Judæus apella!
> "Non ego."

This, I think, must be left to the maintainers (if there
be still any such) of the literal accuracy of the Jewish
histories. The story, then, of the forcible restoration
of Zednanref by the triumphant Niatirbites vanishes,
like that of his forcible detention.

What the real facts of the case were, it may not be
quite easy to determine: but the following appears at
least a *probable* account of them.

We have heard already of the fears entertained by
the princes of Eporue lest their subjects should follow

the example of the Ecnarfites. Those fears were not
groundless; and we may well suppose that the people
of many states were struck by the vast advantages
which the Ecnarfites had reaped from their revolution. Amongst these we should reckon the people of
Niaps, though there was doubtless a strong party in
that country who adhered, with bigoted tenacity, to
the old *régime*. Tumults and confusion were the consequence. Zednanref, ignorant (as his education had
left him) of the mode of managing liberal institutions,
found himself incapable of dealing with this trying
crisis: he retired into Ecnarf, and placed himself under the direction of his best friend, Noel-Opan, where
he might have a safe opportunity of watching the op-
eration of the new machinery, as guided by such a
master-workman. Meanwhile (unquestionably at
Zednanref's own request) Phesoi, the brother of
Noel-Opan, was sent to undertake the administration
of affairs in Niaps. Hereupon the disaffected champi-
ons of tyranny spread a report that their lawful king
was kept a prisoner by the perfidious ruler of Ecnarf,
and took arms, in pretended assertion of his claims.
The efforts of Phesoi were nevertheless crowned with
a fortunate issue; and the slanderous story was in due
time refuted by the reappearance of Zednanref, who
came back unshackled by any conditions, and with
full liberty to act as he pleased. The first act of the
grateful monarch was to disavow all participation in
the base calumnies which had been circulated to
blacken his magnanimous benefactor. He *confirmed*
Phesoi's officers in their places, and imprisoned or
banished those who had traitorously abused his name,
and whom Phesoi had nobly declined to punish by his

own authority. Zednanref's conduct, then, appears (when the truth is seen) to have been as wise and honourable, as it seems base and infatuated in the narrative of this blind partisan. But the chronicler calculated his story for the meridian of Niatirb; or perhaps only gave currency to the traditional legend which he found there received.

The story which comes next, about the burning of the Niatirbite merchandise, I was at first inclined to reject as a mere fiction—"a weak invention of the enemy." But a curious fragment of what seems (from its feebler and more prolix style) a later continuation of these chronicles, has since come into my hands, which shows, I think, that *it*, too, may have some historical foundation. The fragment is this: "There were merchant-men in Niatirb who traded to the land of Anich, and had large traffic with it. They went thither in ships, and brought thence very costly merchandise—even bitter herbs. For the Anichims love the bitterness of those herbs, and steep them in water, and drink thereof. But the Niatirbites love it not; but they put sugar therewith to sweeten it. So the merchant-men went, year by year continually, to the land of Anich for the bitter herbs; and gave in exchange money, even gold and silver, in great abundance. And the profit of their traffic was great; and the merchant-men grew rich exceedingly.

"Then those merchant-men said among themselves: Behold our silver and our gold goeth out unto Anich, and returneth not again, and we bring nothing thence but only these bitter herbs. Moreover the Anichims enhance the price on us, so that we shall be impoverished. Go to: let us bring them hardware, and articles of curious workmanship. Peradventure they will take them in exchange.

"Then those merchant-men took hardware and articles of curious workmanship, and brought them to the land of Anich, and set them before the Anichims. But the Anichims answered them, and said, Nay, but we will have gold and silver.

"Then the merchant-men said among themselves the second time, Go to, let us try them with broad cloth and with fustian, and with divers kinds of cotton goods, and of woollen. But the Anichims answered them the second time, Are not the silks and muslins of Anich better than all the broad cloth and the fustian of Niatirb? And they laughed them to scorn.

"Then the merchant-men were sore grieved; and they said one to another, Behold, these two times they have refused our goods: What shall we do therefore?

"Then rose up a certain wise man and said unto them, Try them yet a third time also, and take unto them opium, peradventure they will choose *that*. Now opium is a drug, which, when a man tasteth, he becometh mad or foolish, and pineth away, and dieth miserably.

"As soon, then, as they had set the opium before the Anichims, the men of Anich answered and said, Behold, now this is good: We will give unto you our bitter herbs for opium; and, if that be not enough, take ye of us also gold and silver, as the price thereof shall be.

"So the merchants were glad when they heard that; and they brought out opium in their ships year by year, and sold it to the Anichims; and the

Anichims took it, and they became mad or foolish, and pined away, and died miserably.

"Then the king of Anich was exceeding wroth, because his people died miserably, and he sent letters unto his rulers and officers saying, As soon as these letters be come unto you, go presently and burn up all the opium that is in the land, and destroy it utterly. So the rulers and officers made diligent search, and burned up all the opium that was in the land. Howbeit, there was some left, which the rulers and officers had hidden for themselves in secret places.

"Now the queen of Niatirb was a just queen, fearing God and doing uprightly. When, therefore, she had heard of all that the king of Anich had done, she sent forth ships of war and valiant men, and very much artillery, to waste the land of Anich, and to take the cities thereof, because of the opium which the king of Anich had burned.

"Also the priests of the land of Niatirb, which did eat at the queen's table—(she is lady over them, and they have a tenth of all the increase of the land. Howbeit, they receive not the full tenth)—arose and said, Behold, the Anichims shall be subdued before our lady the queen, and the trade of the merchantmen shall be restored, which the king of Anich hath cut off: let us, therefore, now send men unto the land of Anich, to teach the Anichims that they be not drunken with opium as heretofore, neither give it unto others that they may be drunken. For it is a law of the Niatirbites, held in reverence by all the people, that whatsoever thing they would that men should do unto them, they should do unto others likewise. Then the queen said, Send, and I will also take cities from the king of Anich, that the men whom ye send may dwell there safely, and teach the men of Anich the way of uprightness."

This story is, no doubt, monstrously absurd. The costly merchandise of *bitter* herbs, fetched in ships from a great distance, for the purpose of being *sweetened* at home; the pious zeal of the good queen and her priests (who have a right to the tenth, and yet, with the characteristic modesty of the holy tribe, do not take a full tenth)* to teach the Anichims not to *use* the poison they were forced to *buy*—are sufficiently ludicrous. But, if I am not wholly mistaken, this substratum of fact remains—*that the* Niatirbites *poisoned the goods which they imported into* Anich. I am willing to allow some weight to the character here given of the queen. She was probably no worse than her predecessors. At any rate, she was A WOMAN, and, therefore, naturally merciful. She would not, therefore, have supported this nefarious scheme, if it were not a part of the established policy of her country. As to the excellent law of practice which is said to have been held in reverence by the Niatirbites, it is plain that the priests must have expounded it as referring to private individuals exclusively, not to the public policy of states and princes.** In all ages, in-

---

*On the antiquity of tithes, see Selden and Spelman. The first notice we have of *tithes* occurs in the case of Abraham, who, as Daumer has proved, certainly came from America.

**At any rate, the Niatirbites no doubt reverenced it as an *excellent rule for the* Anichims. So many consider universal toleration the plain duty of all—except the true believers. And the republicans of Kentucky confine their constitutional dogmas "all men are born *free* and equal," to the *whites*. Indeed, the

deed, casuists have held a distinction between these two cases; and not only Hobbes and Machiavelli, but Christian divines, have stretched the license of sovereigns very far.

If then, as we may now assume, the poisoning of merchandise was an established part of the state craft of Niatirb, we have a very reasonable account of Noel-Opan's conduct in burning their wares, and exhorting his allies to follow his example. If we reject this account, we must suppose that this man, who had risen by his own talents to the chief place among a free and great people, was really no better than a fool!

But why, if the goods were poisoned, did not Rednaxela, ruler of Aissur, follow the example of Noel-Opan? This may seen an objection: but, on a closer survey, it will prove a strong confirmation of our view. The fourth chapter will disclose to us the machinations of that wily sovereign so clearly, as to leave no doubt of his having throughout played a double part; and affected a sort of friendship for Noel-Opan, while he was really in league with his implacable enemy. The goods, then, imported into Aissur were *not* poisoned; because Rednaxela had a secret understanding with the king of Niatirb: and the refusal of Rednaxela to burn the Niatirbite merchandise was rightly taken by Noel-Opan as an acknow-

----

great difference between the Northern and Southern portions of the United States leads me to suspect that the population of the latter is not so much of British as of Niatirbitish origin. My friend Professor Sillyman of Massachusetts has accumulated a great mass of evidence on this subject, which, it is to be hoped, he will soon publish.

ledgement that such an understanding subsisted. These multiplied confirmations, as it appears to me, place the hypothesis of the *poisoned merchandise* beyond all reasonable doubt.

I am disposed to allow that there may be a considerable amount of truth in the account of Noel-Opan's campaign against the Aissurites. We must, however, make large allowances for the warm colouring of a prejudiced narrator. There is, however, this mark of veracity to be recognised, that he allows Noel-Opan to have been victorious in his conflicts with human enemies. That he was ultimately obliged to retire before the severity of a Northern winter* is no impeachment of his military prowess. As Philip II. said in a like case, He waged war with men, not the elements. But that his retreat was not the total rout which is here described, is plain from the fact that we find him again immediately in the field at the head of a great host. Armies cannot be conjured up in a day by an enchanter's wand. There is also a manifest piece of falsification in representing Rednaxela's subjects (the slaves of a despot!) as literally *forcing* their sovereign to refuse conditions of peace. The object of that myth is transparent. Its design is to represent the government of Noel-Opan as even still more odious to the people, than to the

---

*Aissur, or Aissour, may be the region from which the *Missouri* (אִישׁוּר סִי *mei-aissur*—"the waters of Aissur") takes its name. It is clearly part of "the north country." Aissurpi, again,—i.e. אִישׁוּר פֹ, "the mouth of Aissur."—would suit the geographical position of *Texas*.

princes of foreign states,—how truly, we have already seen.

It is quite possible, indeed, that Rednaxela may have drawn his unguarded enemy into a treaty, for the purpose of detaining him till winter, and then made the pretended violence of his subjects an excuse for breaking it. This would be quite in keeping with that monarch's character.

I must, however, do the chronicler the justice of observing that, in one place, an injury has been done him by the transcribers. Monstrous as some of his legends are, he could hardly have meant to say, that "the *Aissurites* set fire to Vocsom (their own capital!) and burned it." *Aissurites* is here plainly a mistake for *Ecnarfites*. The word had occurred so frequently in the preceding sentences that the sleepy copyist unwarily substituted it here, where it makes nonsense of the passage. I do not, however, undertake to maintain the truth of even this corrected statement.

CHAP. III.

The sovereigns of Aissurpi and Saturia appear to have been encouraged by the reverses of Noel-Opan to resume their old hostility. It is remarkable, however, that, in the account of this formidable confederation, we find no mention of the king of Niatirb. The restless enmity of that monarch, no doubt, made him willing enough to join in it; but the late infamous affair of the poisoned merchandise (in which he

showed himself ready to sacrifice the lives of his
former allies for the sake of wounding Ecnarf through
their sides) had probably so disgusted the other rulers
of Eporue, that they declined his scandalous assistance. In his place we have a recreant Ecnarfite, the
ruler of Nedews,—bribed, as we shall see presently,
to this base act, by the gift of a province wrested
from Kramned.

In this war misfortune seems again to have attended the Ecnarfites. Noel-Opan's army, thinned by
the calamities of the Aissurite campaign, was probably now not numerous enough to cope with the overwhelming masses of the combined despots. Stratagem
of some perfidious sort, seems also to have been employed. I say of *some perfidious sort*;—because the
chronicler betrays uneasiness in describing it, by
having recourse to a daring falsehood. He represents
Noel-Opan as deliberately breaking down all the
bridges *but one* behind his own army. If he had said,
that this heroic chief broke down *all the bridges*, we
might possibly credit the story. Such things have been
done by military commanders to inspire their armies
with the courage of desperation; though the Ecnarfite
soldiery seem not to have belonged to that class
which requires such mean stimulants to valour.* But
to break down all the bridges *but one*, would have
been the act of an idiot. It would have manifested at
once that he was in *meditatione fugæ*, and yet designed to make his retreat as disastrous as possible.

---

*Ethic. Nicom. iii. 11. καὶ οἱ πρὸ τῶν τάφρων . . . .
παρατάττοντες· πάντες γὰρ ἀναγκάζουσιν. δεῖ δ᾽οὐ δι᾽
ἀνάγκην ἀνδρεῖον εἶναι, ἀλλ ᾽᾽ ὅτι καλόν.

This, I say again, is incredible. If Noel-Opan had
not intended to retreat, but in case of defeat, to
perish, like the Spartans at Thermopylæ, on the field
of battle, he would have broken down *all the bridges*.
If, on the contrary, he had contemplated a retreat, he
would have desired to bring off his army as safely as
he could; and, therefore, would have broken *none*.
The story refutes itself. But such lies are not forged
gratuitously. Fixing *blame* upon Noel-Opan betrays a
consciousness that blame must be fixed *somewhere*.
We may consequently assume that it was not by any
legitimate manœuvre, but by some perfidious stratagem, the bridges were broken down in the rear of the
Ecnarfites: and, casting our eye upon the immediate
context, we instinctively recognise the traitor. "Then
the king of Airavab, whom Noel-Opan had made king
of Airavab, came out to stop the way against the Ecnarfites." Can there be a doubt that it was through
the treachery of this man (who was probably left to
guard the passes) that the bridges were broken down
behind the great captain of the Ecnarfites?

Still, amidst all his unmerited misfortunes, the
genius of Noel-Opan appears to have triumphed: and
the terms of peace which he finally arranged, though
they dimmed his personal splendour in point of out-
ward rank and power, secured to Ecnarf the solid
good she had long struggled for; while, to all thinking
men, the greatness of Noel-Opan in his retirement, of
generous self-sacrifice, must have seemed more sub-
lime than when in the zenith of his success. The
chronicler, of course, would have us believe that
Noel-Opan surrendered at discretion. But his own
facts refute him. By his own statement it appears that

Sivol II. was restored upon condition of leaving the Constitution of Noel-Opan intact, and renouncing all his brother's political connexions. The hateful "laws and ordinances of Niatirb," which Ecnarf had so long resisted, were abandoned for ever. The interest of that odious power had declined even amongst its ancient (and in some respects *natural*) allies. Circumstances had smoothed the way for a general pacification: and Noel-Opan, perceiving that he alone was an obstacle to this desirable conclusion, magnanimously laid down the power which he had unambitiously assumed. He had taken it for the good of Ecnarf; he resigned it for the good of Ecnarf. Let the reader pardon me if I seem to speak warmly. Every honest heart will feel, and every ardent one will express, a kind of exultation at rescuing a great character from the fang of calumny. The present case reminds us of the case of Niaps: and what we then proved confirms (I think irresistibly) our account of the transaction before us. We have to deal with the same falsehood,—only somewhat more carefully elaborated.

If further confirmation were needed, it would be found in the remaining part of the chapter. It cannot be believed (at least by any but a Niatirbite intellect) that, if the rulers of Eporue had really thought Noel-Opan the ambitious and oppressive monster whom this historian paints him—"a tyrant and a murderer"—they would, now that they had him at their mercy, deserted by his own subjects, and reduced to beg compassion from his enemies, have put him in possession of Abel, or given "silver and gold" to his mother and brethren! We know them by this time rather too well to credit such rash generosity on their part. Let me observe too, that, in the MS. already mentioned, of these chronicles, I find a marginal gloss upon the word Abel, to this effect: "Behold, it is nigh unto Akisroc, and lieth in the sea, as thou sailest towards the sun-rising." This is an important fact. Noel-Opan withdrew, it appears, to the scenes of his nativity. Probably, Abel was the larger—from its name,* we may add, the more fertile—island, upon which Akisroc depended. In this case Noel-Opan would have had the satisfaction of guiding, in his declining years, the fortunes of his own country, and receiving, amidst his patriotic cares, the recollections of his youth.

I pass over the incidental notices of Noel-Opan's domestic affairs. We have not, perhaps, light enough to judge of these private transactions. Like some other illustrious persons, he seems to have been unfortunate in his wives. But the less we meddle needlessly with the ladies the better; otherwise one might remark that, proposing to himself tranquillity in the close of his life, Noel-Opan may not have grieved very much that he saw the face of his second wife (*the daughter of the ruler of* Saturia) no more.

---

*אבל "locus graminosus pascuum." *Gesenius.* Compare the Arabic اٻل. It occurs in the names of places. 2 Sam. xx. 14; Numb. xxxiii. 49; Mich. vi. 5; Judg. xi. 33, &c. The expression in the gloss, "towards the sun-rising," leads us to the etymology of Akisroc. It was considered the last island of the *west*, and more properly connected with the *east*. Hence its name, אחי־זרח (achi-zroch), "the brother of the sun-rising." This favours the idea of its being a dependency upon Abel.

CHAP. IV.

I need hardly pause to observe that the chronological arrangement is not exactly followed in this chapter, which plainly refers to the times of the last campaign against Noel-Opan, immediately before his retirement. It is a highly important piece of history, and throws much light upon the crooked policy of the king of Niatirb, and his base associate Rednaxela.

According to the chronicle, this latter prince is described as, first concerting with Noel-Opan the employment of the Kramnedite ships *against* Niatirb, and then *assisting* Niatirb in its unjust detention of those very ships. Such conduct, even upon this statement, would be perfidious enough; but it is too absurd to be believed. The chronicler seems to have little regard to the character of Rednaxela, and paints his meanness in its true colours; but, in order to screen the villainy of the king of Niatirb, he throws in a spice of fatuity which spoils the compound. Knaves, indeed, are often fools *in the long run*; but they are not mere idiots. Noel-Opan, we may be sure, never published or owned any design upon the Kramnedite navy; so that the only evidence of this pretended secret plot between him and Rednaxela, must rest upon the testimony of the latter,—the confession of an avowed *particeps criminis*. No jury ever convicted the meanest culprit on the uncorroborated declarations of a guilty informer; and we cannot admit this impudent assertion as sufficient to implicate one, whose character has hitherto stood the test of very severe examination. This pretended league was a convenient pretext for a bold act of tyranny; and, applying to the case the reasonable criterion of *cui bono*, we must determine that the king of Niatirb (who reaped the profit of the story) was the original inventor of the lie; in passing which he met with ready assistance from the frontless impudence of the unblushing Rednaxela.

Kramned being thus disabled by the seizure of its fleet, the ruler of Nedews thought he had a good opportunity of partaking in the spoils. It is evident that he had previously bargained for the connivance of the other powers, and that Yavron was, in fact, the price of his treachery to Noel-Opan. If the Yavronites had been misled into the belief that the king of Niatirb was a friend to freedom, and had assisted the Niapsites to obtain it, they were now undeceived; and the conduct of that infamous prince (even on the representation of his own partial chronicler) in the present instance, is so inexpressibly base and cruel as to leave no doubt that I have throughout given a fairly drawn picture of him. Next to that of vindicating a hero is to be ranked the pleasure of detecting a scoundrel.

I do not pretend to clear up all the perplexities which involve the mysterious person who figures under the name of Apap. How the Ecnarfites should have been "servants to him" it is not easy to understand. But etymology* will favour the conjecture that

---

*P and B being interchangeable, I take Apap to be equivalent to Abab, a reduplicate of אב, *father.* Compare the Greek πάππας. The whole of Eporue may have been originally one state, and Apap the lineal representative of its ancient sover-

he may have held some titular pre-eminence among the states of Eporue (a vestige of old patriarchal connexions)—in some respects analogous to that of the German emperors in mediæval Europe. The more ferocious nations of Niatirb and the "north country" spurned his innocent traditionary claims to respect; which were gently acquiesced in by the milder Ecnarfites. Hence the rude people of the north described the southerns as his *servants*. We have already learned from the history of Zednanref (a key which unlocks many difficulties) the true meaning of a *captivity in Ecnarf*. Apap had found an asylum in that country. His restoration appears to have been one of the points insisted on by Noel-Opan in the general pacification; and the princes of the north, knowing that Apap was "an abomination" to their subjects, were obliged to colour their unpopular act of justice as they best could, by representing it as done to spite the Ecnarfites. If the story, after all, could not be made very consistent, that was not their fault.

CHAP. V.

We may dismiss this chapter without much ceremony. It is a pure myth from beginning to end: probably the work of some later legendary, who was

---

eigns. So to a very late period, and after the house of Timour had really nothing left them but a small territory round Delhi, the coin, throughout the whole of what *was* their empire, was struck in the name of the Great Mogul. The position of the later caliphs would furnish another analogy.

desirous of giving to the Niatirbites the whole glory
of finally crushing Noel-Opan.* *They* had, as we have
seen, no share in the great combination of princes
which led to his retirement. It was, therefore, requisite that he should be brought upon the arena once
more to receive the finishing stroke from the *miseri-
cordia* of the king of Niatirb. In other respects, this
second subjugation of Noel-Opan is a mere repetition
of the former;—just as Rebecca's adventure with
Abimelech is a counterpart of Sarah's, in the harem
of Pharaoh. A great battle, ending in grievous
slaughter of the Ecnarfites: the flight of Noel-Opan to
Sirap: the eagerness of the populace to "thrust him
out;" his banishment to an island,** and finally the
tranquil re-establishment of Sivol II. on the throne of
Ecnarf. *Ovum non ovo similius.* Homer's unhappy
warriors are most unceremoniously resuscitated,
when some hero's glory demands that he should
"fight his battles o'er again," and "thrice slay the
slain." But Noel-Opan's return from Abel and second
banishment, will only be received by those who expect the grand Avatar of Prince Arthur, "rex quon-
dam, rexque futurus," or those *similar mythic fig-
ments* which may be found in most popular creeds.

Qui Bavium non odit amet tua carmina Mævi

---

*It is in fact what the immortal Strauss calls "a glorifying
myth."

**The expression, "another island," is important, as a dis-
tinct admission that Abel was an *island*.

Let the reader observe how many marks of the genuine myth here combine:—

1. The miraculous*** complexion of the events. Noel-Opan returns with 600 men! Immediately all Ecnarf submits, and Sivol flies without striking a blow. Noel-Opan is defeated *in one battle*; and immediately the Ecnarfites thrust him out. Sivol returns as rapidly as he fled; Noel-Opan *chooses* to surrender to his greatest enemy, the king of Niatirb. It is really like the changes of a Christmas pantomime.

2. The expectation that a great person, whose actions have deeply impressed the public mind, should return, is a common phenomenon. And such expectations (as in the case of the Jewish Messiah) often produce a belief in their own fulfilment.

3. The honour of Niatirb *required* this appendix.

4. The story is worked up from the materials of older legends.

***A second law, observable in every event, is that of succession: even in the most violent epochs, in the most rapid changes, a certain order of development may always be remarked; everything has its origin, its increase, and its decrease . . . . In fine, when we take into account all the psychologic laws, we cannot believe that a man should, on any particular occasion, feel, think, or act otherwise than as *men ordinarily act*, or as they themselves would have acted at another time."— *Leben Jesu*, § xvi.

5. It is inconsistent with the previous narrative.

a) In *that*, Noel-Opan was thrust out as a murderer and a tyrant: In *this*, he is received with open arms.

b) In *that*, Ecnarf had just lost three great armies successively: In *this*, after less than a year's space, Noel-Opan is able to raise, in that same country, another army, large enough to fight a desperate battle with the fresh troops of Niatirb, Aissurpi, and Muigleb.* Unless, indeed, we suppose that Noel-Opan encountered the combined host with his "600 men who drew the sword."

c) In *that*, Noel-Opan's settlement in Abel is made freely by the assembled princes *for the purpose of removing all danger of his further interference*: In *this*, the place and circumstances seem so badly chosen that he is able to recover his throne in a few months.

d) In *that*, the king of Niatirb is his most hated enemy. While other princes seem disposed to deal mildly with him, and are "merciful kings;" especially the king of Saturia, with whom he is connected by marriage. In *this*, he chooses to surrender

---

*Gleb may be the lost radical of the Latin *Gleba*. Mu (*i* is only a syllable of composition) connects itself with the Hebrew מִי, מִן, and the Coptic Mo, *water* (Jablonsky opusc. t. i. p. 152). Hence we have *Mu-i-gleb*, "the watery soil:" probably the *alluvial deposit* of the Sacramento or Amazon rivers.

to the king of Niatirb; who, instead of keeping him (as he easily might) in Niatirb, sends him to a distant land, *for the sake of being obliged to maintain a fleet of ships to guard him.*

e)   In *that*, Noel-Opan always *flies* when he is left with only a small force. In *this*, he trusts himself to the people who had just driven him away with 600 men!

If this story be not a **myth**, where are myths to be found?

APPENDIX.

ON THE SATURIANS.

Some remarks connected with this important point have been communicated to me by a learned friend, Professor Sillyman of Massachusetts, which I here subjoin in the shape of an *Excursus*.

"While fully admitting the identity of the Satyrs of Greek history, and the Saturians of these chronicles, I prefer the old Shemitic etymology סתר *abscondit*, to that suggested by my ingenious friend, Mr. Newlight. We may, I think, trace that etymology to an old legend preserved by Zarate, (*Discovery of Peru*, t. ii. p. 49,) which relates that some of the people of South America were compelled to take refuge, from a great flood, in *caverns*. Hence they may, in memory of their deliverance, have assumed the title of Saturians or Troglodytes.

That the Satyrs were really of American origin, appears incontestably from many considerations.

1. We have in Ælian (*V. H.* iii. 18) an account of a conversation between Midas (the gold-seeker) and Silenus, the chief of the Satyrs. The statements there made by the Satyr are manifestly a description of South America, mixed up with some mythical interpolations. Let the reader judge. "He said, that Europe, Asia, and Libya,

were only islands surrounded by the ocean; but that the true *continent* (῞Ηπ·ειρον, cf. Eporue) was that which *lies beyond this world.* He declared its magnitude to be immense, . . . and that there were many and great cities in it. . . . That there were two principal ones, the *warlike* and the *just*, (compare the language of the chronicler with respect to Ecnarf and its rivals) . . . that they have great plenty of silver and gold, so that iron is more valued there than gold, &c."

Here then, I think, we have plainly a Saturian's own account of his own continent.

2.   The Satyrs are expressly called by Hesychius, Δευκαλίδαι. Now there can be little reasonable doubt that the story of the Noachic or Deucaleonite deluge had its origin in the knowledge of the founders of the Semitic race having come from America, emerging from

The world of waves, the sea without a shore.

The original name of (at least a part of) America was, as Daumer has proved, Noah. That the Semitic races derived their origin from Noah, was the genuine tradition; which was disguised by the myth in question. In later times again, the mythic dove (Columba NoÆ) gave occasion to the fable of *Columbus*; just as the true etymology of the name America—אם עדוגה, "the Mother of *Flowers*," suggested the story of *Amerigo the* Florentine.

3. Bacchus (whose story Huetius[*] long ago detected in the myth of Moses) was probably the hero-leader of a Saturian colony. Plutarch, indeed, (*Sympos.* lib. iv. quest. 5, p. 671,) has pointed out at large the conformity between the Bacchic and Jewish solemnities; and the distinct statement of Montesinos (given by Manasseh Ben Israel in his *Spes Israelis*, Amstel. 1650) respecting an essentially Jewish race, speaking an essentially Hebrew language, in South America, has been often laughed at but never refuted. The popular reader will find a pretty accurate but grossly prejudiced account of the matter in Basnage's *History of the Jews*, book vi. chap. 3. An American origin may be traced clearly in the myth of Moses being so called because taken out of *an ark floating in the water,*—the established symbol of an American colonist."

THE END

---

[*]*Demonstr. Evangel*, Prop. iv. e. iii. § 3.